Falling From a Pink Cloud

A Memoir

FALLING FROM A PINK CLOUD

WHEN SPIRITUALITY LEADS TO A DEAD END

BY
M. L. FRANCOEUR

Readers and journalists can reach Michel L Francoeur at fallingfromapinkcloud@gmail.com

All rights of reproduction, translation, and adaptation are reserved for all countries. No portion of this book may be reproduced in any form without written permission from the author except as permitted by copyright laws.

ISBN:9 781069 094414
Copyright © 2024 by Michel L. Francoeur

Contents

CONTENTS i
IMPORTANT NOTES iii
ACKNOWLEDGMENTS iv
PREFACE 1
CHAPTER 1 3
CHAPTER 2 9
CHAPTER 3 17
CHAPTER 4 27
CHAPTER 5 37
CHAPTER 6 45
CHAPTER 7 53
CHAPTER 8 61
CHAPTER 9 67
CHAPTER 10 75
CHAPTER 11 83
CHAPTER 12 89
CHAPTER 13 99
CHAPTER 14 109
CHAPTER 15 119
CHAPTER 16 129
CHAPTER 17 143
CHAPTER 18 151

CHAPTER 19	159
CHAPTER 20	165
CHAPTER 21	175
CHAPTER 22	183
CHAPTER 23	191
CHAPTER 24	199
CHAPTER 25	205
CHAPTER 26	213
EPILOGUE	221
NOTES	225

IMPORTANT NOTES

This book critiques certain new religious movements and cults. The excerpts from the catalog of religious teachings are made to comment on and criticize them. Also, certain passages in my text may be shocking for some readers—I needed to tell them and expose my truth, which is similar to that of many who have grown up in such environments—be advised. For reasons that will become obvious as you read through the chapters, most of the names of people I interacted with have been changed. However, all the facts recounted in this book are truthful to the best of my knowledge.

ACKNOWLEDGMENTS

I'd like to express my heartfelt appreciation to everyone who supported and encouraged me throughout this book project. All my admiration also goes to those who have shared their doubt, struggles, wisdom, and experiences through writing. Their stories have provided me with many insights and gave me inspiration, to find my own voice.

PREFACE

*"Knowledge is acquired through experience.
Everything else is just information."*
Albert Einstein

    I was born into the Mission of the Holy Spirit, a highly controversial French-Canadian new religious movement. Luckily, my parents removed me from there when I was around five years old. However, a few years later, they introduced me to Scientology, another New Religious Movement already labeled as a cult at that time. I attended Scientology's organizations regularly for almost twenty-five years before leaving it definitively in my mid-thirties. I then continued my search for meaning in other religious movements, such as the Brahma Kumaris, another sectarian New Religious Movement I frequented briefly before ending my chaotic journey a few years later within an evangelical church in a sorry state.
With this book, I aim to address a situation that persists unchecked in Quebec and elsewhere, affecting many people: the impunity granted to certain New Religious Movements that are often considered cultic and denounced by former members and numerous specialists in the field.
    I am neither an investigator nor a journalist, and I do not hold a university degree. My thinking is based primarily on my personal experiences, which I consider sufficient to justify my

position regarding the place we give to the 'religious field' in our societies. Understand that while I talk primarily about my experience in this book, its subject concerns us all, as the education an individual receives, whether religious or not, will influence their relationships and actions toward others.

With this in mind, I aim to shed light on this 'overly shadowed' area of our societies and discuss the impact that religious indoctrination and certain transcendental practices can have on a person and their loved ones.

CHAPTER 1

CORNERED

October 2016

For some time now, I hardly sleep at night. I spend hours turning in bed, juggling with my body and my thoughts. To capture what comes to my mind in these restless moments, I keep a notebook and pen on my bedside table, jotting down notes I plan to revisit the next day. I try not to get out of bed every time an idea strikes because my priority is to get some sleep. This chronic insomnia started a few weeks ago. It was a Sunday early in September, after attending a particularly disturbing religious ceremony at church with my wife. The day before, I had helped with a car wash organized by the church's men's committee to raise funds for an orphanage in Haiti. The activity, which I had proposed and pushed for, was tainted by an unfortunate incident that sparked tension between one of the church's influential members and me. Mr. Barde, a church employee, had approached my fellow washers and me, claiming we weren't working fast enough and that we weren't cleaning the cars properly. His intervention struck me as both demeaning and unnecessary. I told him that we'd been working since morning, and none of the motorists had seemed dissatisfied with our efforts. We were volunteering, after all, putting in our time and energy without pay. Frustrated, I ended my response with a tone that matched my irritation: "Wash them yourself if you prefer!"

Sadly, things unfolded just as I'd feared. When I joined that church a couple of years ago, I expected there would be conflicts and differences of opinion with other members. I'd been part of more than one religious movement before this one and often had bad experiences. In the beginning, when I attended the Sunday services, I kept my distance, resolving not to get too involved with any church committees or with Christians who have different views regarding Christianity. Even if I did get involved, I promised myself I wouldn't tolerate the same treatment I had in the past in other religious movements I had frequented. I wasn't there to be bullied by some church leaders, and I wouldn't let anyone step on my shoes. However, they would make me pay for it. Let me be clear: I admit I was a bit harsh with Mr. Barde and another member, Mr. Grelot, a few weeks before. But I never imagined that men who claimed to be disciples of Jesus would act as they did that Sunday morning during the service.

A month earlier, when I got out of bed that Sunday morning in September 2016, I felt great. I was proud of what we had accomplished the day before at the car wash. It meant a lot to me because, for the past couple of years, things had gone from bad to worse. In the last two years, my father, mother, and one of my brothers passed away. Additionally, I had recently lost my job and was struggling to find another. Having become a father for the first time in 2014, I was desperate to stabilize my finances, pay off my debts, and plan for my family's future. However, my efforts weren't yielding results, and I was on the brink of bankruptcy. So, the carwash felt like a victory. It was as if the tide was finally turning in my favor.

I was especially proud because fundraising was my idea. I had even insisted on speaking at the men's committee meeting to propose it. In doing so, I clashed with an older church member, Mr. Grelot, who seemed to get offended every time I spoke. Still, the event's success proved that my idea was solid, and I was glad I had pushed to make it happen. I couldn't wait to celebrate with those who participated and hear how much money we had raised. When I arrived at the service, I greeted a few people before heading to the back of the church with my wife, where we usually sat with friends. Surprisingly, as we were about to settle in, Mr. Grelot approached us and invited us to sit in the second row, right in the center of the assembly room. Just behind my friend, Pastor Gaston, who would be preaching that day. Taken aback by the offer, I started to wonder if Gaston had arranged this to congratulate me in front of everyone for organizing the carwash. When he heard my voice as I spoke to my wife, Gaston turned and gave me a blank stare. Still excited to see him, I smiled, convincing myself that he was probably just nervous about preaching.

The musical period started, led by musicians I didn't recognize. They were good—the kind of talent we usually brought in for special occasions. I joined the rest of the assembly in singing the familiar songs, my voice full of enthusiasm. Grateful for finally feeling better after months of struggles, I raised my hands to the sky, thanking God as I awaited what I thought would be my 'moment of glory.' I had been somewhat depressed for a while, and a little recognition would have meant the world to me. After the music, we moved to the announcements. To my surprise, Gaston himself stepped forward to deliver them, a task usually handled by one of his assistants. He started by discussing the carwash, clearly pleased with the results. He then began to thank the people who had helped, naming them individually, starting with those seated in the back. Sitting in the front, I waited patiently for my turn. Given how he was singling out everyone, I expected the same treatment. After all, I was right there in the center of the room, having been invited to sit up front. However, when Gaston got to me, his tone changed. He stopped the individual thanks, looked at me even colder than before, and said, *"When a brother pitched the idea of a carwash, I wasn't convinced. But we still went ahead..."* I was stunned. "A brother?" I thought. What did he mean by that? Gaston knew my name—he had just listed everyone else by name. How could he forget mine, especially when I'd been in his office at least once a week all summer, chatting with him? The realization hit me hard: he hadn't forgotten but was deliberately ignoring me, withholding the recognition I had been so sure was coming. So, I quickly told myself, mustering all the resilience I could find, that I would surely benefit from a lesson in humility. I knew that I sometimes spoke loudly and disturbed others with my exuberance, that I had been intolerant recently, and that my refusal to address Gaston as Pastor, seemed rebellious, even though I had good reasons to. I remained calm and showed no emotion, as I had learned to do in Scientology, while Gaston started delivering a disturbing sermon inspired by the fall of Satan: *"At the beginning of creation, Satan was in heaven with all the angels and archangels. He was God's favorite angel— flamboyant and charismatic, playing sublime music. However, one day, he tried to rebel against God and lost. He was then banished from the heavenly realms. As he left heaven, he took half of the angels with him..."*

Gaston was vigorously declaiming, sometimes looking at me directly in the eyes with anger. I was deeply impressed by the sermon, which drew on specific passages from the prophet Isaiah and the Apocalypse of John to describe the fall of Satan. I felt as though I was being singled out. According to the sermon, Satan would have been expelled from paradise after his failed attempt to overthrow God and reign over the universe himself. Gaston delivered the sermon with intense enthusiasm, occasionally locking eyes with me in a way that felt accusatory. Petrified, I told myself I should have spoken more softly to Mr. Barde. That I should learn to hold my tongue and that I got what I deserved. I, like Satan before me, had now fallen from grace! At that moment, I realized my time in that church was over, and I eagerly awaited the moment I could leave that place. As my wife and I were leaving the room, we ran into Mr. Grelot, who said, *"Michel, Mr. Barde would like to see you before you go!"* Surprised, I waited for the man I had argued with the day before at the carwash, though all I wanted was to leave that cursed place as quickly as possible. When Mr. Barde finally stood before me, he looked at me strangely without saying a word. I asked what he wanted and he replied with a satisfied smirk and a slightly petty tone, *"Oh, nothing in particular. I just wanted to see your face before you leave!"*

At the moment, I didn't understand Mr. Barde's gesture. I thought he was just being odd. However, everything became clear later that day. He had spoken to Gaston about our disagreement during the carwash, who then planned to correct me that morning and push me to leave the assembly after causing me pain and humiliation. I was stunned. Images flashed through my mind: Mr. Grelot surprisingly inviting me to sit in the second row, the intimidating looks from Gaston, and his targeted remarks, careful not to mention me by name—finally, Mr. Grelot's second intervention and Mr. Barde's arrogance before I exited the church hall. The three of them had conspired to execute this Machiavellian plan to undermine me. It was a blatant attempt to manipulate me, using coercion to strip away my free will and break me!

That night, I couldn't sleep as my thoughts and feelings clashed like marbles in my head. I couldn't articulate what I was experiencing, and it was disconcerting. All I knew was that I felt deeply disappointed and angry at Gaston, whom I had considered a friend. In the morning, convinced that the knot in my stomach I'd felt all night was due to the large piece of sugar pie I'd eaten after supper, I discussed it with my wife. Viewing it from a different perspective, she helped me realize that the pie had nothing to do with it. My discomfort was a result of the events that had occurred the day before. Deep down, I knew she was right. However, I had encountered similar situations before and had learned to ignore them. In those cases, I made it a habit to tell myself that my opponents were imbeciles who didn't deserve my attention.

Yet, this time, it was different. For a few days, I could barely sleep. What I had initially mistaken for indigestion soon evolved into daily anxiety attacks. After a few weeks, I began to fear that these symptoms might worsen and develop into severe mental disorders. This fear drove me to question my condition and grapple with existential concerns. Luckily, in the following weeks, I engaged in thorough self-reflection that gently guided me toward recovery. Although I wouldn't come out of that misadventure unscathed, my insomnia and anxieties proved beneficial, leading me to undertake deep introspection. That event had created a breach within me, allowing my suffocating unease to finally express itself. From then on, I would start listening to that little beast inside my chest, who sometimes took control of my life without warning and made me lose all diplomacy.

I began searching for answers to my questions: Why was I so upset? Was it the betrayal, the rejection, or the disillusionment? Was it the discomfort I felt from being compared to Satan in that sermon? Or was it the realization that I wouldn't return to that church, where I had thought I could help other guys like me and where I had made a few friends? I couldn't pinpoint exactly what had shocked me so deeply. However, I understood that I needed to find the answers within myself and stop looking elsewhere. As I turned forty-five, I realized I was repeating the same pattern as my father before me, shifting from one religion (or cult) to another and bringing my family along just as he had. Helpless, I felt trapped in that pattern and had to find a way out. My "quest for meaning" had led me to a dead end.

In my search for inner well-being beyond myself, I had unwittingly opened my mind to anyone who offered me attention and had embraced eccentric and potentially dangerous doctrines, sometimes propagated by narcissistic individuals. One of the first things I did was to stop attending any religious or self-improvement movements. I also discontinued my studies in Pastoral Counseling at the Bible college, which I had undertaken intending to work alongside Gaston—the very person who had metaphorically stabbed me in the heart.

Overall, I decided to break the silence, reclaim my story, and speak openly about the negative impact that the various religious movements I had encountered in my life had on me. I would no longer accept the unacceptable and would take responsibility for warning others about the inherent dangers of joining certain groups or engaging in specific self-improvement or religious practices.

CHAPTER 2

MY ANCESTOR'S RELIGION

At my father's funeral, which took place about nine months before the car wash, I took one of the photos offered as mementos for visitors. I brought it home and placed it on a piece of furniture next to my television—something every good son would do. However, every time my gaze fell on the photo while watching a movie or TV show, I felt a surge of anger, regret and sadness. To address this, I moved the photo to the door of my refrigerator, hoping that my resentment toward him would fade on its own. A few months later, as I was retrieving something from the fridge and saw his portrait again, I felt the urge to move it out of my sight. My negative feelings toward him had not waned. Seeing his face filled me with bitterness, sadness, and disappointment. I wanted to forget and move on with my life. For that reason, thinking it would help, I threw my father's photo straight into the trash. However, realizing that my two-year-old son had witnessed me discard his grandfather's photo filled me with immense shame and made me feel like a coward.

Even though my little boy didn't grasp the whole meaning of my gesture, I couldn't help but think that he might do the same with a photo of me one day. So, I retrieved the picture from the trash and put it back on the fridge. This incident between my son and me intensified my inner turmoil, making me increasingly intolerant toward those who showed me little regard.

I thought I was handling my father's departure normally, as much as one can define normality in grief. I assumed that after a while, his shadow would fade, and my life would take a different turn. But in reality, I couldn't make peace with him or let go. I was still caught in conflicts with my father that had long preceded his absence. His values, such as racism, misogyny, and homophobia, which clashed with my mentality, led to many disputes between us. Even though I wanted to move on, too many questions and frustrations held me back. I harbored painful memories of him, who was no longer with us, and it saddened me deeply because it was too late to change anything about it.

Over time, as I spoke with people who had known him, I realized that my opinion was unique to me. Many people cherished my father and had fond memories of him. Gradually, I began to reconsider my opinion and came to understand that many of the arguments between us were a result of being his descendant. He had special plans for my life, plans I had refused to follow, and despite my intentions, I had deeply disappointed him. From that point on, I began to distance myself and gave him the benefit of the doubt. I decided to learn more about his background and the context in which he had started his family. I wanted to understand the origins of his ideals, which I had been so resistant to. Perhaps then, I could forgive him and someday even consider putting his photo back in my living room.

To begin my search, I wanted to remember my childhood, when my father was more often present at home. I knew that, like my parents and grandparents before me, I was born into a controversial religious movement known as the Mission of the Holy Spirit, commonly referred to as "The Mission."

It was a subject we rarely discussed at home. My father and mother had divergent opinions about it; she called it a cult, while it drove him to madness. My sisters, brothers, and I regularly attended the assembly hall of that cultic new religious movement. However, I only have a few memories from that time. One I recall quite clearly is of a festive assembly on April 17, the founder of this movement's birthday, a man named Eugene Richer, who later called himself Eugène Richer dit Lafleche, here in Quebec, Canada. He also lived under the false names of Joseph Manseau in Fall River, Massachusetts, and later as John LaFleche in North Los Angeles, where he died on January 12, 1925. To simplify things,

I'll refer to him by the name on his birth certificate, Eugene Richer, throughout this book. During the ceremony, we drank grape juice in front of the platform before the assembly's servant laid hands on our heads. I also recall a comedy show held in the same room on Everett Street in Montreal, where one of my father's cousins, another individual named Lafleche, who, like me, later joined Scientology at my father's invitation. I remember laughing at his jokes regarding zombies living in hell.

Another fond memory is of a large fair organized in the communal gardens of the low-income housing complex where some Mission's families lived. That day, Mom allowed us to join the picnic, as several of the children at the party were from The Mission. And since we were on the verge of leaving it. I see myself again, around three or four years old, frolicking with about ten other children, a piece of tomato pizza in one hand and a glass of juice in the other. It remains one of my oldest memories.

In 1973, when I was two years old, a particular atmosphere began to settle at home following an announcement made during an assembly of The Mission. It was predicted that a major disaster, such as a Third World War, would soon occur, potentially leading to the near extinction of humanity. This prediction followed a supposedly prophetic dream reported by Emmanuel, one of the sons of Gustave Robitaille, who succeeded Eugene Richer until he died in 1965. Emmanuel, who was considered a medium, warned the people in the assembly that the disaster would begin the following year, in 1974.

Due to the lack of upheaval, The Mission began to fracture into several groups. The following year, some of the preachers, named 'servitors,' witnessed The Mission implode from within. One of them that I know of, Gilles Francoeur, one of my father's uncles, established his branch of The Mission. A significant number of members followed Emmanuel Robitaille, who had likely fabricated the dream to undermine his father's movement, with whom he had always been in conflict. They joined him in converting to Jehovah's Witnesses.

Although not everyone was swayed by the warning, many of the faithful took the dream seriously. The announcement of these major tribulations led to severe consequences for many. Some sold their homes and businesses, often at a loss, to have cash on hand for provisions and to relocate their families far from big cities—a few even built underground bunkers.

In 1975, we moved to Mascouche, a small town located northeast of Montreal, into the countryside. My father found a large house that fit his limited budget. Were my parents moving us away from the city to escape the predicted tribulations? Probably, as they stored barrels of dry food in the basement in case we needed to stay isolated for a while. I remember the dried vegetables, the barley, and, above all, the dreaded black-eyed beans. I hated those beans, which my mother prepared in various sauces and tried to make us eat despite the global upheavals that never materialized.

Then came 1976, and nothing significant happened, at least in Quebec, except for the Summer Olympic Games in Montreal. Before the warning, the Mission's membership was between 2,000 and 3,000 members. In the years following the warning, around 1,400 members left. Several couples who had met in The Mission separated after leaving the movement. Families, sometimes with more than a dozen children, found themselves in difficulty. In discussions with some fathers who left The Mission, it was clear that their children had suddenly become a burden. They had been strongly encouraged to have as many children as possible, but the reality proved too much. Fathers like mine found themselves with a large number of children 'on their hands,' as they put it.

My parents officially decided to leave The Mission probably because they felt betrayed, seeing that nothing dramatic was occurring. I was about five or six years old. At that time, my father was twenty-eight, and my mother, who was pregnant with our youngest sibling—the eighth child—was thirty years old. She had given birth to all of us within nine years and also experienced five miscarriages during that period. Leaving The Mission was salutary for my mother, who then chose to deliver the youngest in a hospital after having the other seven children at home. She was in such poor physical condition that the doctor who assisted with her last childbirth apparently warned her that she would not survive another home birth. Like many other members of The Mission, my parents did not join any of the various assemblies that emerged after the collapse of the leading group. Despite leaving the movement, my father never stopped believing in Eugene Richer. This was evident from the photo of the 'master' holding a pipe, which remained on one of his walls long after we had ceased attending the 'rooms' of The Mission.

Apart from a few childhood memories related to The Mission, I do not retain much of the teaching I received there. I set out to research this new religious movement to understand the type of education my parents received within it—education that could have shaped their belief system and instilled in my father values to which I had remained indifferent. I began by searching the Internet, hoping to find information about this movement. I quickly came across articles denouncing it as an apocalyptic, isolationist, and misogynistic cult that keeps children isolated from the outside world, which is said to be under Satan's influence. However, I could not find any books or documents that would help me learn more about the foundational beliefs of this movement.

To dig deeper, I contacted several relatives who had left the movement at the same time as my parents. These former members were not eager to revisit their painful past. They mostly referred to the movement they were born into as a cult and seemed irritated when I mentioned its name. I then reached out to a friend of my father, whom I had met a few times, who was deeply involved in the movement. On the phone, I expressed my interest in studying the doctrine taught at The Mission. Surprised, he initially questioned my motives, but after my explanation, he admitted that he had cleared out almost all the documents he once had. Nonetheless, he sent me some old newspaper clippings he had carefully preserved in a drawer, intending to use them one day to denounce the movement he had once been highly involved in. One of these articles, published in Le Petit Journal in 1969 by G. Asselin, provided more information about the founder of The Mission. It read:

> "In 1894, Eugène Richer, the founder and spiritual leader of The Mission, was suspended from his duties as a police officer in the same year he began serving with the Montreal police under the number 99. He faced accusations of pimping. Richer was released on bail during his appearance and quietly disappeared."

In reality, Eugène Richer did not go far. He stayed with Adela David, whom he married in 1895, until she sought a divorce and separation of property in 1903. In her petition, Madame David accused him of physical abuse, including kicks to the stomach and punches to the face and head, in front of their eight-year-old daughter. She also claimed he had threatened to kill her and requested the court to seize their property to prevent him from leaving her penniless.

The same article by G. Asselin noted that in 1923, Eugène Richer was in the French-Canadian colony of Fall River, Massachusetts, under the pseudonym Joseph Manseau. According to the journalist, Richer faced legal trouble again in Massachusetts for fraud and gross indecency, as he occasionally delivered sermons in a "transparent nightshirt." He disappeared from Fall River, only to reappear two years later in California, under the new pseudonym John La Flèche. He died on January 10, 1925, at the age of 53. The article also revealed that several other members of The Mission ended up in prison, notably for fraud. Clearly, Eugène Richer was not the only criminal in the group!

Curious, I continued my search for more recent articles online. One, published in La Presse in 2002, caught my attention. It reported that in 1996, The Mission of the Holy Spirit faced legal action:

> "In 1996, a Superior Court judge ordered a woman, a member of The Mission of the Holy Spirit, to stop exposing her two children (ages 8 and 9) to the religious group."

Another article, published in Métro in 2015, quoted a young woman who had recently left The Mission of the Holy Spirit. Her statement touched me deeply. She said, "*I left because there was no way I would raise my children there.*"

At the start of my search into The Mission, I promised myself to remain objective and not be swayed by the opinions of a few detractors who might seek revenge by denigrating their former religious movement. I still had several cousins in this group, and I wasn't going to rely solely on a few journalistic accounts to form an opinion about my ancestors' religion. So, I continued searching for other sources of information about this movement. On the Internet, I found only one site dedicated to The Mission of the Holy Spirit: the one from the Saint-Paul-de-Joliette branch, the faction founded by my father's uncle, Gilles Francoeur. It was the only group publicly represented online in 2017. Upon arriving at this site, I encountered a term I didn't understand: eugenics. I looked it up in the online Larousse dictionary and found:

"*Theory seeking to operate a selection on human communities based on the laws of genetics.*" The site of the Saint-Paul-de-Joliette group gave this definition:

"*The possibility for humans to give birth to children with a natural propensity toward goodness and virtue, even from ordinary people. Eugène Richer dit Laflèche teaches that Eugenics and the Imposition of Hands are the only ways to remove sin from the world, drive out death, and bring about lasting world peace.*" [1]

According to what I read on that same site, Eugène Richer also suggested that women bore primary responsibility for the future of humanity:

"*The woman gives birth to the teaching of her spirit. Only the impressions and state of mind of the mother affect the quality of the soul incarnated in the fetus. Therefore, she is the origin of the quality of our society. The pregnant woman is like a KODAK camera, capturing and immortalizing what strikes and impresses her. Similarly, the woman gives birth to what touches and impresses her.*" [2]

If I understood correctly, the woman is held responsible for the spiritual qualities and behavioral attitudes of the child she brings into the world. But what role does the father play, aside from being the progenitor?

"Often the closest person physically and morally, and therefore most likely to impress the pregnant mother, the father must strive to create an atmosphere of peace and evolution. He should aim to surround his wife with beautiful things so that she can conceive happy and spiritually evolved children." [3]

I continued reading and began to grasp the reasoning behind this religious movement:

"What The Mission of the Holy Spirit recommends: This view of the importance of the procreator's state of mind led Eugène Richer dit Laflèche to stress the importance of high-quality teachings (especially spiritual) and experiences for pregnant women. He advocated for encouraging the cultural and spiritual development of women to enhance the quality of the child to be born." [4]

From what I read, the primary goal of The Mission was to bring consecrated children into the world, starting from gestation, overseeing the environment in which the pregnant mother lived. At first glance, I saw nothing particularly destructive in this plan for humanity's regeneration presented by The Mission of the Holy Spirit, which involved creating structured family units where parents carefully supervised the child's upbringing. All in all, at this stage of my investigation, I thought that while establishing clearly defined family roles might seem monotonous and disheartening—especially for women—I did not see any wrongdoing in The Mission. I would need to dig deeper to uncover any potential issues.

CHAPTER 3

ANOTHER BELL RINGING

The information I found online about the Mission of the Holy Spirit left me unsatisfied. Questions continued to plague my mind. For instance, I wondered why my parents, along with several other members of my extended family, had chosen to leave this movement in which they were born into the third generation. There must have been a reason for that. From what I had read till then, The Mission had little to criticize beyond the sacrifices it demanded from its members to regenerate future humanity; I did not see any particular harm in it. So! Why hadn't my parents joined one of the new groups that emerged after the warning? Were they too cowardly?

Answers to my questions came quickly. Having given the movement a chance by reading its proposals, I now wanted to explore the perspective of those who denounced it. I refined my search by adding the term 'cult' after 'Mission of the Holy Spirit' in the search engine. New sites appeared, and I decided to review some critical articles, particularly one from the French website of the UNADFI, the National Union of Associations for the Defense of Families and Individuals Victims of Cults. Their 2017 website presented a markedly different story:

"The Mission of the Holy Spirit propagates a misogynistic ideology: women must be submissive and docile. The letters of Eugène Richer contain violent and contemptuous remarks,

asserting, for example, that women (whom he referred to as 'female dogs') are all suffering from chronic infidelity and, by definition, are unworthy of the support provided by their husbands. (...) Followers are encouraged to marry young and have many children, many of whom are named Eugène, Eugénie, Richer, Richère, Laflèche, Flèche, Fléchanne, in honor of their founder." [5]

Conflicted about my stance on The Mission, I wanted to understand more about the doctrine they taught. For that, I needed to go beyond the Internet and find religious documents published by this group. I sought to judge for myself what they had taught my parents. Eventually, I obtained the 801-question questionnaire, a voluminous document used to instill The Mission's doctrine in children growing up within the movement. It was formatted in a question-and-answer style for memorization. I found the most revealing information within the Mission of the Holy Spirit's Questionnaire.

This document served as evidence in a trial before Judge Georges Audet of the Superior Court of Quebec in 1996, intended to expose the religious indoctrination inflicted on children within The Mission of the Holy Spirit. It is attributed to Gustave Robitaille, the heir apparent of Eugene Richer. The following questions and answers are from this questionnaire. For the sake of accuracy, I have retained the original spelling used in the text.

Question 1

What is the Holy Spirit?

The Holy Spirit is God.

Question 2

What does the word God signify?

The word God means: 'Sweet Light'

Question 3

How many PERSONS are there in God?

There are three PERSONS in God.

Question 4

What are the names of the THREE PERSONS in God?

Jehovah, Jesus Christ, EUGÈNE RICHER DIT LAFLECHE.

Some of the words in the questionnaire were capitalized to highlight important concepts. for the children of The Mission. It was clear, from the initial questions, that Eugene Richer was presented as the third person of the Trinity, the Holy Spirit. It was through him that the regeneration of the kingdom of God on Earth was expected to occur.

Question 23

What must we receive to be the Son of God?

We must receive the Consecration.

Question 24

What do you mean by consecration?

Consecration is the Baptism of the Holy Spirit.

Question 25

How is the Baptism of the Holy Spirit applied?

The Baptism of the Holy Spirit is applied by the IMPOSITION OF THE HAND ON THE HEAD.

Farther in the questionnaire, I learned that, according to The Mission's teachings, Jesus was consecrated in Mary's womb by the angel Gabriel, who would 'sent' to give humanity an 'example.'

Question 30

What was the Angel's salutation?

> *Hail Mary, the Lord is with you, and Jesus, the fruit of your womb, is Blessed.*

Question 31

> *Who brought the Blessing to Mary for the fruit of her womb?*

> *It was an Envoy of God by the name of Angel Gabriel.*

In The Mission of the Holy Spirit, Christ was therefore considered to be the first of the 'consecrated children,' nothing more. According to The Mission's teachings, children born within the movement who received consecration in their mother's womb by Eugene Richer or one of his servants were in the process of becoming 'similar' to Jesus Christ.

Question 50

> *Who is the savior of mankind?*

> *The Savior of mankind is the Holy Spirit. (Eugène Richer dit Laflèche).*

For The Mission, Eugène Richer was the Holy Spirit and the savior, meaning that Jesus was only the example. And what about God in all that?

Question 51

> *The Holy Spirit being God, what is God?*

> *God is Nature.*

Further in the questionnaire, Eugène Richer or Gustave Robitaille used familiar images like the sun, moon, and sea to make their corrupted vision of God's world more tangible.

Question 67

> *Are poisons, tares, injurious herbs, toxins, mortal minerals, etc., also the work of God or Nature?*

> *No. They are the work of Satan, the spirit of badness and death.*

Question 68

In that case, Satan is also a creator?

Satan hasn't and can't create anything; he engenders or corrupts God's work.

According to The Mission's teachings, the world had willingly surrendered to Satan due to humanity's 'disobedience' by a God who would have done this simply to satisfy His ego!

Question 69

Didn't God know that Satan was out to corrupt His work?

Certainly! That is the reason why He carefully warned our first parents not to listen to the temptator symbolized under the aspect of a serpent.

Question 70

Then why did God let Satan do it?

It was to better manifest his glory and power.

Thus, 'the God of The Mission' would have abandoned humanity to Satan, who would have made the Earth his domain, and all newborns who had not received intrauterine consecration within The Mission, his children. This was disturbing and far from the understanding I had of a loving God.

Question 74

Is this Satan unique, alone, or does he have a body, a family?

He is "legion," says the Gospel. Also all children who are born from human doctrines are HIS children.

Question 75

What evidence do you have of this?

Didn't Jesus not say, "You have Satan as your father, the devil..."

As with many cults, the author of the questionnaire distorted biblical teachings to support his agenda. He avoided placing the biblical quotes in their proper context or interpreting them correctly. For instance, the quote from John 8 used for Question 75 was addressed to Pharisees who opposed Jesus. Similarly, the teaching about the angel Gabriel coming to save Jesus by laying his hands on Mary's womb does not align with biblical scripture, regardless of one's belief in the scriptures

To take my mind off the questionnaire, I read other documents from The Mission's catalog, such as the Ceremonial of the Consecration:

"My brothers, through this consecration, the work of my hands and your ministry is to accomplish the Reign of the Father on Earth. I will no longer pray for them or for you, for my Father is and will be in you for time and eternity. And my Father, who sees you and hears you, cannot refuse you anything because you carry His Name within you." [6]

This extract from the Ceremonial sounded appealing, especially to the 'consecrated children.' However, as I read further, the cost of attempting to escape one's role in The Mission was revealed to be enormous:

"But woe to him who would attempt to receive this consecration without the nuptial robe, that is to say, with bad dispositions and who would be tempted to turn back! For my Father wants us to be one in Him as you are to be one in Me, without division, for outside my Way is darkness, condemnation, and hell for eternity." [7]

What I read there was even more disturbing than what I found in the Questionnaire. The spell that accompanied the consecration within The Mission of the Holy Spirit was clear: "Stay with us, or go to hell for eternity!" was written in black and white in their religious document. I also remember being told that we, who had left the Mission, would reincarnate into vermin such as cockroaches or rats.

"Spells are communication phenomena. A message is sent that takes the form of a prophecy, but its mere utterance ensures that this 'prophecy' will be realized automatically. For example, if parents say of a sulking child, 'This child will have a bad temper later,' they risk reinforcing their own negative expectations and thereby shaping the child's future behavior to fit their prediction. A spell weighs on him! The future will naturally prove the parents right... Dominique Megglé, psychiatrist and hypnosis specialist. [8]

Reading these texts, I began to understand the dilemma my parents faced. They who had given birth to eight consecrated children of the fourth generation who were supposed to become like Jesus.

"The Master revealed that 'It would take three to four generations of attention before all vestiges of evil are gone from the flesh.' [...] 'Eugène Richer dit Laflèche taught that Eugenics and the Imposition of Hands constituted the only means of removing sin from the world, chasing away death, and bringing about lasting world peace." [9]

My parents had only two options: to stay in the movement or leave to join the 'world' of Satan, bringing their children with them. The stakes were enormous, assuming they believed in the doctrine of The Mission. With the next question, I understood one of the reasons why the consecrated children were not encouraged to attend schools of 'the outside world.'

Question 111

Who shall teach and instruct those children?

They won't need any teaching from anybody since the 'Light,' the real one, will have enlightened and instructed them before birth, and the 'Nature,' which comprises all, will abide in them.

Consecrated children were said to reason more intelligently than adults, like Jesus, who was already teaching at twelve!

Question 311

You do not admit that old men are wiser than children?

When one is not wise at birth, one never becomes wise. Jesus confounded the Jewish theologians and doctors, among which were men of old age, and He was only twelve at the time.

The person who wrote the Questionnaire had no shortage of imagination when it came to giving the world outside The Mission the 'colors' of Satan. They impressed the children with all sorts of fabrications about the 'outside world' to scare them and keep them within The Mission.

Question 180

What does the word "sun" signify?

This word comes from "sol" (e), which means BASE, foundation, heel, foot; there is also a certain resemblance with the word "solus", which means alone, solitary.

Question 181

That's impossible because the sun is above in the highest constellation therefore, it cannot be the base or the foundation that is supposed to be on earth.

The sun isn't above, but below; it is the foundation of all our planetary system. It is the fire of hell that reflects hypocritically in space.

Question 182

Is the sun truly a star or a symbol?

It is not only a vain symbol, only a burning reflection.

More shocked by what I was reading, I remembered a summer afternoon from my childhood. That day, my mother took us to the park. The sun was high, with not a cloud in the sky—the burning midday sun reflecting off everything. In my memory, I saw Mom again, sitting on a bench, exhausted, looking sad and depressed. As I recalled that day, several questions surfaced: Did my mother believe all this nonsense? Was it the idea of an 'infernal star' reflecting the fires of hell on her consecrated children—now considered children of Satan—that made her so sad? Did she worry about what our destiny would be? Or did she miss the community she had grown up in, along with her brothers who stayed in The Mission, our uncles who would only see us in an assembly hall? Or was it all these factors combined that left her in such a miserable state?

To distract myself from that sad memory, I thought back to one of the rare joyful moments I had with my father when I was young—the only time he played with me as a child. With my eyes closed, I could see us in the street, in front of our house in Mascouche. It was hot and bright. That day, my father took me on his shoulders, even though we were on a bicycle. I was thrilled, unaware of the danger, as he let go of the handlebars. I could see Mom panicking while my father laughed, just like me, perched on his shoulders, laughing loudly, sharing a moment of pure joy and complicity with this Dad I loved so much! It was a connection I would seek over and over but rarely found during my childhood. Most of my early memories revolved around my mother, who stayed home to watch over us. Dad was always working. At least, that's what he told us!

CHAPTER 4

CHILDHOOD MEMORIES

Early in life, I developed the habit of wandering off alone. One summer morning in 1976, when I was about five years old, I decided to visit my father's cousins, who lived roughly a mile away in the same neighborhood. I walked there, making sure I stayed on the side of the road while the hot sun was shining over me. When I arrived at my destination, I was greeted by a large Saint Bernard, panting happily with its tongue hanging out. However, I was quickly sent home - manu militari -by my little cousin's mother, who already had enough of her dozen children and had no time for me.

Later that autumn, after one of my first days of school, I told the bus driver I had permission to have dinner at a classmate's house and that one of my parents would pick me up later. I lied. I also told my friend's mother that my parents knew where I was, which was also false. That evening, for the first time in my life (though not the last), the police brought me home after my mother contacted them, frantic because I hadn't gotten off the school bus. That's how I began reaching out to people outside my home, a habit I don't think my mother ever appreciated.

Yet that same summer, she finally allowed us to hang out with people outside The Mission. I'll never forget the day she told me, "You can go, Laflèche! Play with that boy on the other side of the street with his big trucks! We're no longer in The Mission." For me, this moment marked the end of our time in that movement. Even today, I can clearly picture the two of us playing in the pile of sand in front of his house—those images are tinted with a halo of happiness and freedom. Freedom that I quickly embraced as life at home became increasingly stifling. Leaving The Mission sent my mother into a depression that would last forever; nevertheless, despite everything she would have to go through, she remained mostly functional for us kids.

Question 198

Why did the Master get married? Jesus didn't...

Jesus couldn't marry a female of this world, because He was born of God. There wasn't anywhere on earth a woman, a suitable companion of his own sort: All of them being females, none of which were real women, in the real sense of the word.

According to The Mission's teachings, every person on Earth, except for those consecrated during gestation, were children of Satan. That's why Jesus remained single and why people in The Mission married only among themselves.

Question 199

Which would mean that the Divine Lord E.R.L. did meet a genuine woman possessing a divine character?

No more than Jesus.

Question 200

Then God was united to a beastly female with a beastly character?

Absolutely.

I was floored! Eugène Richer, the 'God' referred to in that last question, used the term "beastly female" when describing a woman—his spouse! That said a lot about the character of the leaders of this new religious movement.

I then began to question the sanity of Gustave Robitaille, who wrote this indoctrination document inspired by his Master's teaching and of those who taught it to children. When I read the next question, I was even more stunned. After reducing the sun to a reflection of Hell, hypocritically reflecting in space, the document presented the moon in a way that left me speechless. I had to reread the questions several times to fully grasp them. The author described the moon as a mirror, reflecting both the woman's uterus and the world of sinners in which we supposedly lived.

Question 298

The astronomers will never believe what you affirm because, for them, the moon is a cold star, traveling at some 290,000 miles from Earth.

As to being a cold star, it is possible. Because most women are frigid, even frozen with their husbands and hot with their lovers. This star, which we believe up there in the firmament, lives, wanders, acts, and above all, sins here on Earth.

Question 299

What we take for granted as a celestial star called the moon, what is it really?

Only an image. The moon is the picture of the female and, at the same time, the surface of the earth… it is simply an image of maternity with its various phases. It is the mirror, or, if you prefer, the living picture, the astral picture of conception, of pregnancy or plenitude, and of parturition or decline.

To understand the next questions, one must know that the face of Eugène Richer apparently appeared on the lunar surface. He, being 'one with nature,' was even recognized with his pipe in his mouth!

Question 321

If the Master hated the Moon, why then did He show Himself in it?

To teach the woman what she should do and does not, namely: Bear the Holy Spirit in her entrails instead of the Evil

Spirit, which she confines in her womb and envelops in with a mortal flesh, which flesh is subject to microbes, to bacteria, to worms and holds the Thermo Bacterium or germ of death, which it transmits to its children. All sinners, whoever they are and whatever their names may be and whatever denominations they may belong to, are children of Satan.

Question 322

Explain yourself.

If all the children that are born have hidden faults and vices, invisible at their birth, but develop themselves with the age, it then means that their mother conceives them of a vicious, revolted, and contaminated spirit. That spirit it's Satan. The birth of a sinner proves without ever a doubt that the mother is herself a sinner.

Question 323

You undoubtedly mean to say that the woman conceals the Spirit of Evil in her womb?

Absolutely! This makes Satan the father of this humanity…

Growing more upset with each question, I realized that Eugène Richer and Gustave Robitaille deeply hated women. Sitting in front of my screen, I thought of my poor mother, who had died a few years earlier, and of all the young girls who had to memorize this doctrine, which depicted women in such a horrible way. I was disgusted. Trying to imagine myself in the place of one of these girls broke my heart made me sick. It became painfully clear why most of the women I knew who had left this cult had no fond memories of their time in the movement: they must have been traumatized.

I also understood why women in The Mission were forbidden to breastfeed their children—they feared transmitting the '*Bacterium Thermo*,' the so-called germ of death mentioned in Question 321.

Eugène Richer dit Laflèche and Gustave Robitaille, as further evidenced by other writings collected in The Mission's documents known as "Les Propos," were misogynistic psychopaths: – *"Satan is the work of a woman."* – *"The Woman, Mistress of the demon, foul cesspool."* – *"Our enemy: woman."*

At this point, I started to believe that the 'religious education' of this movement had instilled misogyny in my father from a young age. I also began to refer to The Mission of the Holy Spirit as a cult, just as my mother had.

While reading other texts, including one titled Le Consolateur (The Comforter) and another called Letters from the Prince, I understood that my father's racist tendencies likely had roots in The Mission as well. The group propagated particularly degrading views about people of color:

"If we haven't yet found a detergent, soap, or acid capable of whitening the skin of a n..., we've also not discovered a baptism capable of cleansing the sinner, born of Satan." – *"About monkeys, the Master once said, while gazing at a n..., "You know, Gustave, there's some monkey in there."."*

At this point in the questionnaire, I was convinced that The Mission of the Holy Spirit should be denounced as a dangerous cult. Its teachings were not only contemptuous but also harmful to society at large.

I was nearing the end of the questionnaire, but the surprises weren't over yet. I had just noticed that members of The Mission regarded the Catholic Church as a sworn enemy—something they avoided at all costs. Given the Church's pervasive presence in Quebec until the 1970s and even into the 1980s, this could only have led to severe social isolation for The Mission's followers.

Question 675

That is your opinion, but what proof have you that the pope is Satan, Hell's monarch?

> *Is it not true that once Lucifer transported Christ, in spirit, showed him all the kingdoms of the earth from the summit of a high mountain and offered them as present to the Son of God, on the condition that he worshipped him. Well, in order for the Devil to offer thus the earth to anyone, it must first belong to him.*

The document stated that water baptism was a grand deception designed to place newborns under the yoke of Satan. Even more shocking was the claim that the Pope himself was none other than Lucibel—the spirit of the Prince of Darkness incarnated as an angel of light!

At the start of the journey that would become the writing of this book, I initially intended to explore the extensive collection of documents associated with The Mission. However, the thought of delving further into this man's misogynistic and antisocial ramblings made me sick to my stomach. Thanks to my parents, I was no longer entangled in this new religious movement, one that had already caused enough suffering in my childhood. I decided to leave it behind.

Nevertheless, I couldn't resist reviewing an article[10] written in English by Susan J. Palmer, a controversial[11] Canadian sociologist known for her defense of cults, and Dale J. Rose from the Department of Religious Studies at the University of California, Santa Barbara. The article centers around a historical document[12] that holds key information, shedding light on the origins of The Mission of the Holy Spirit. According to the authors, the sect began within a Catholic prayer group dedicated to the Virgin Mary, which Eugène Richer and his older brother, Israel Richer, frequently attended.

Palmer and Rose recount the statements made by Israel Richer after prophetic visions he claimed to have experienced in the Sanctuaire du Très Saint Sacrement, located on Mont-Royal Street in Montreal, Quebec, Canada. There are also excerpts from letters Israel tried to personally deliver to the Pope. In these letters, he requested, among other things, that the Vatican recognize his theory. He argued that a woman's uterus must be purified and the child baptized before their first breath in the world, which he described as ruled by Satan. He sought approval for the creation of a new lay religious order that would perform this unique form of baptism. After the Vatican rejected his requests, Israel returned to Montreal empty-handed, only to discover that his brother Eugène, a man with little formal education but extraordinary charisma, had already begun establishing a new religious movement without waiting for Vatican approval. Thus, between 1914 and 1917, the Mission of the Holy Spirit was born. Israel, however, eventually sided with the Catholic Church, bringing back several members of the prayer group to the Catholic church.

In 1927, Gustave Robitaille, Eugène Richer's heir apparent, turned The Mission into one of the worst misogynistic cults America has ever known. Today, the movement consists of five or six assemblies, mostly located in the greater Montreal area, with an outpost in California. These assemblies often argue over several issues but share common views regarding the nature of women, the world outside the Mission, and their disdain for the Catholic Church and its Pope.

When I began researching The Mission, I promised myself I would keep an open mind. However, the more I learned about this movement and its teachings, the harder it became to remain detached. I grew upset, realizing that people belonging to that new religious movement were allowed to teach such doctrine to children. From then on, I looked at my parents with more compassion, appreciating the courage it must have taken for them to pull us out of what was essentially a sect of the Catholic Church at the time their grandparents joined The Mission, which had now become a dangerous cult.

I can only imagine the deep disappointment they must have felt when they abandoned what they believed to be a grand rescue mission for humanity. A mission they truly believed in and into which they had invested much of their lives, even starting a large family for its sake. The shock of disillusionment must have been tremendous.

I've also started to understand the roots of some of the longstanding conflicts between my father and me. Particularly the ones about my involvement in musical performances at various Catholic churches. And, of course, the argument that erupted when he found out I was going to marry a woman of dark skin.

I had now reached the final page of this fiery rant, known as the Mission's Questionnaire: an attack on women, the Catholic Church, and the world at large. The final questions of the document left me stunned. The author seemed to have poured all his energy into ending it with an absurd flourish. He compared women to the raging sea, threatening to swallow the boat of Jesus' disciples as they crossed to the other side. His grotesque writing took a verse from the Bible and twisted it to land yet another blow against women.

Question 799

I admit to not understanding.

In the primitive Church, the priests strived to observe the recommendations of the celestial, Jesus. They walked, as their Master, upon calm seas, but as soon as the influences, which sprung up from the woman (sea) began to rise, those successors of the Galilean phony were frightened and sank into the bitter liquid of transgressions and crimes.

Question 800

Therefore, most of the bad influences, that is to say, the pernicious and disturbing winds, come from the woman?

I would dare to say all; for the mother impregnates in her fruit sentiments which never erase themselves. She is the terror of the Apostles, who cowardly yield before her feminine fits of anger. (...). Next to the priest, who conducts and instructs her, she is responsible for all the terrestrial transgressions, for all the political upsetting. All those who fear her, fatally sink in the whirlpool of her waves.

Question 801

But Jesus saved his disciples by offering them a helping hand?

Yes! it's effect, by the imposition of the hands, the sole ministry recognized by the divinity, that the Lord will operate the rescuing of the maternal wracks.

While revising my text, the thought of giving up crossed my mind. I kept telling myself that now that I understood where my father came from, I should've been able to forgive and move on. Then, while browsing the Internet, I came across an excerpt from Louise DesChâtelets' column in Le Journal de Montréal, a popular French Canadian newspaper. What I read, written by someone who had once been part of a cult, reignited my determination:

"*My parents, who began their adult lives in the 1970s, forced their three children, including me, to be part of the same cult as them. It took me becoming an adult myself to realize the harmful effects on my balance of their religious madness. I left this religious practice at the end of my twenties, but it seems that, with regularity, morbid thoughts return to pollute my existence. I would really like to get rid of all these crazy ideas that still come back to haunt me, even though my parents are deceased, and I remain convinced that I made the right move by fleeing the cult.*"[13]

It confirmed that if I wanted to understand why I ended up in that state in that church, I had to dig deeper into my past. I needed to rethink my life from the ground up to figure out why I kept finding myself in these situations. And for that, I had to keep writing.

CHAPTER 5

FACING 'THE WORLD'

During my very first days of class in a small primary school in Mascouche, I quickly noticed that the mere mention of my first name, Laflèche—meaning 'the arrow' in French—sparked excitement among those unfamiliar with The Mission. Imagine calling someone 'the table' or 'the car.' While Laflèche is often a surname or the name of a town, within The Mission, it was given as a first name to honor the master, Eugène Richer dit Laflèche, or, perhaps, to 'label' us. For me, that name became a burden. I despised it from the start and still do today. I longed for a common name like my classmates had—one that would allow me to fly under the radar once in a while.

Fortunately, at that little school in Mascouche, I discovered music classes. From the first note I played, I found a joy and passion that would stay with me for life. Another souvenir I remember vividly from Mascouche happened around the same time. That day, Mom gathered all eight of us children around a lottery ticket. There we were, standing in a circle in the living room, holding hands under her watchful eye and that of one of her friends. She told us to close our eyes and pray to God for her to win the lottery. Her expectations were high. I think she truly believed it would work since we were consecrated children.

I believe she bought that ticket hoping to win enough to pay off the mortgage and keep the house in Mascouche since my father had decided we needed to move back to Montreal. Sadly, our 'connection with God' wasn't strong enough. Her plan failed, and soon after, we had to return to Ahuntsic—the same neighborhood we had left just a year or two earlier.

Over the next six or seven years, we would move no fewer than six times. I felt sorry for my poor father, who often shouldered these moves almost entirely on his own and was unable to afford movers.

Back in the city, my parents enrolled me in one of the few Protestant schools available, hoping to keep us out of the Catholic schools that dominated Quebec's education system. It didn't take long for me to realize that even though we had left The Mission, some of its members weren't ready to let us go.

On one of my first days, my older sister, who attended the same school, warned me to only speak to children from The Mission. Mr. Gouga, a school employee and Mission member, was watching us closely. According to the writings of Eugène Richer dit Laflèche, being born into the fourth generation of The Mission made us children of exceptional spirit, destined to build a New World. They wouldn't let us slip away easily. Anyway, I didn't care about their fears of the outside world or their talk of children of Satan. I spoke to anyone willing to listen to me.

From Children of God to Children of Satan

Another childhood memory, one I'd rather forget, comes from a summer afternoon when I was about seven. That day, my father took me and my two older brothers to the countryside to visit one of his sisters, who had stayed in The Mission with her husband and children. They had joined the faction led by Gille Francoeur, one of my father's uncles, after the warning. I can still picture the farmhouse, its rural simplicity, and the large field stretching behind it. We were to spend the night there.

Upon entering my aunt's house, I met one of my cousins, a boy about my age. Naturally, I assumed we'd have the chance to play together. But his mother sent him to bed before showing us where we'd be sleeping, assuring us we could explore the farm and play the next day. The following morning, eager to see the cows in the barn behind the house, I woke up quickly, full of excitement. However, my joy faded fast when I met my aunt, who told me I wasn't allowed to play with my cousin. Apparently, my father had made it clear to his sister and brother-in-law that we wouldn't be joining their faction of The Mission. That morning, I distinctly felt that they no longer wanted us near their children since we now represented the evil that existed in the world.

Genevieve

Around the same time, a woman entered our lives as if sent by an angel to care for us. Geneviève, my mother's first friend outside The Mission, had three daughters who would become like my sisters. That lady would come regularly to our place to help my mother, who was really in need—often overwhelmed, she became stressed and very impatient with us. Genevieve would take us out for activities and picnics, while my mother would do something else in the house or go to an appointment.

Genevieve introduced us to various art forms and encouraged my parents to enroll us in classes, such as swimming lessons or folk dance classes. Without knowing it, she fueled my passion for the arts, especially for music, which had first sparked during my music classes in Mascouche. She nourished the flame that had been lit in me when I played the triangle in class. Under her guidance, I discovered more of my artistic side and began dreaming of becoming a singer like René Simard or Mireille Mathieu.

However, as I imagined myself on stage, a problem emerged in my mind that took my breath away: my first name, Laflèche, that ridiculous label from The Mission that represented a weapon used for hunting and sounded feminine to my ears. How could I proudly stand in front of an audience while the announcer called out my name? "Ladies and gentlemen, please welcome tonight's next artist: Laflèche Francoeur!" I could already imagine the audience bursting into laughter.

One evening, while my father was home, I told him I wanted to change my name to something more normal since I dreamed of becoming a singer. He immediately rejected the idea, insisting that Laflèche was a perfect name for an artist and that it would make me stand out even more. I hated his response and left that conversation feeling frustrated. I never brought it up with him again and never truly came to terms with the name.

Thankfully, I still have a few beautiful memories from those years, mostly thanks to Geneviève: trips to children's theater shows, theater games in our courtyard, and my first movie at the cinema. Her involvement in our lives brought us some of the joy every child deserves—something my mother struggled to provide, likely due to her depression. Without realizing it, Geneviève instilled in me a love for the performing arts, planting a seed that would one day grow into a mighty oak in which I would build a cabin where I would take refuge one day.

She also did a great service to my mother by giving her much-needed moments of respite. Geneviève helped us integrate into society by organizing parties and children's games, which included her kids and other neighborhood friends.

Still, despite her efforts, the atmosphere at home remained heavy. I took every chance I could to get out of the house. I remember wandering alone around the streets near our home or visiting the convenience store across the wide Metropolitan Boulevard when I was just seven. I often begged my older brothers to take me with them on their adventures in the alleys and neighborhood parks. Most of the time, they refused, but my mother would insist, probably because she couldn't stand my crying. So, begrudgingly, they would drag me along on their pre-adolescent escapades, even though I was still only seven.

Petty Crime

Hanging out with my older brothers made me grow up far too quickly. Together, we were always getting into trouble. Up until then, I had been content to run off occasionally to satisfy my thirst for freedom, but in Ahuntsic, I would go much further, diving headfirst into what we called "Satan's world." I smoked my first cigarette with them, hiding in the bushes around the Claude Robillard Center.

Usually, we stole cigarettes from cars or from convenience stores. Sometimes, though, my oldest brother managed to get some with the money we took from the small steel boxes that collected donations at the lanterns near the entrance to Saint-Alphonse-D'Youville church. I'd also gather loose change by lying to passersby, telling them I was lost or late and needed a dime to call my mother or catch the bus home.

That was also the time I discovered marijuana. I wasn't smoking it yet, but I knew what it was. One evening, I remember 'finding' some in my father's pocket. I took it and gave it to my brothers, but they ordered me to put it back. My father had started smoking joints after we left The Mission—small joints, he said, to lift his spirits. He told me years later it was his way of self-medicating. Marijuana helped him keep smiling, overcoming the deep sadness brought on by his departure from The Mission, not to mention the heavy burden of supporting our family. From that time on, my father was less and less present at home. He always returned, though, to rest and to hear the latest from my mother, who did her best to keep us in line.

One autumn afternoon in 1978, she reported about some trouble my brother and I had caused that day. My father decided to punish us with his leather belt. He called us to a small room near the front door, made us drop our pants, and took turns hitting us on the buttocks. It was the first time he had done that, and it didn't go well. In reaction to his outburst, my brother and I ran away that same evening. We walked to the nearby metro station, jumped the fence, and got on the train heading downtown. We wandered through the city until evening, finally making our way to Old Town, determined to spend the night there. After stealing a tablecloth from one of the restaurant terraces in Place Jacques Cartier, we climbed onto the roof of a building, using the tablecloth to shield ourselves from the cold as we leaned against a ventilation hatch. In the middle of the night, freezing and unable to sleep, we climbed back down to find a more comfortable spot. However, police officers spotted us, arrested us, and took us back to the station, where we spent the night in cells. It wasn't until morning that my father came to pick us up. He took us out to breakfast, apologized for hitting us, and asked for our forgiveness. Perhaps he realized that the violence against children, as encouraged in some of The Mission's documents, would only push us further away. His blows weren't going to solve anything; they would only make us turn against him.

Family Christmas

In 1979, now free from the cult, the Francoeur family, to which I belonged, celebrated Christmas like most other families in Quebec! We gathered at the home of one of my mother's brothers, an uncle who, like my maternal grandmother, had temporarily left The Mission. (They both of them would return a few years later.) My mother's only sister was also there with her three sons. There was food, decorations, a Christmas tree, and gifts beneath it. I still remember the game I received from this uncle who hosted the party—he was one of our favorite uncles, though we would only see him once or twice more before he returned to The Mission and cut off contact with us completely.

Our first Christmas together went wonderfully, with the air filled with joy, warmth, and love. In the years that followed, my mother tried to recreate that same atmosphere. Christmas became a special time for many of us. For me, certain hymns like Sainte Nuit, Adeste Fideles, and Oh Holy Night became my favorite Christmas songs—melodies I could sing all year round and that I would later perform during religious services. Participating in these celebrations became very important for our family. It allowed us to feel connected to the society we had now joined.

Unfortunately, since my father couldn't keep up with the mortgage on the house in Ahuntsic, we had to move again the following year—this time to Montreal North. Geneviève, who had by then become almost part of the family, continued to visit and check in on us occasionally. She did her best to help, even though we were often little monsters, testing her patience to the limit. One morning, to express the sense of abandonment I was already feeling, I hid behind a sofa with a large kitchen knife and threatened to cut my wrists if I wasn't given more attention. Of course, I was exaggerating, playing a game with Geneviève. However, she didn't find it funny—she already had her hands full with my younger brothers and sisters.

Sometimes, a friend of my father came to visit us, Michel-George, a man of French origin, a little older than my father. He would practice something he called Dianetic on my older brother. It was intriguing. My father compared it to hypnosis, which was supposed to help people become more intelligent. However, Michel-Georges insisted that it was not hypnosis but therapy.

In the basement of that huge apartment, my father had stored the barrels of dried food he had bought back in Mascouche, dragging them along with us once again after Ahuntsic. We often played hide-and-seek down there, our own 'apocalypse version,' where we searched for hiding spots in case of an atomic war. The atmosphere became so real sometimes that I could almost taste those awful black-eyed beans we'd have to eat again.

Sadly, we wouldn't stay in Montreal North either, and soon we were on the move again—this time to St-Michel, where my life would take a terrible turn.

CHAPTER 6

ST MICHEL

The new neighborhood we moved to was exactly the kind of place my mother had probably wanted to keep us away from when she tried to save our house in Mascouche. In St-Michel, street gangs and drug dealers were everywhere. We were at risk of getting sucked into criminal activities ourselves. While it had been fairly safe to let me wander around in Ahuntsic or Montreal-North, this new neighborhood was a different story. That year my parents separated. My two older brothers and I went to live with my father, while my mother took my three sisters and two younger brothers with her. It wasn't the best situation for me, being stuck with just my older brothers at an age when I wasn't ready for that. To minimize the divide, they found two apartments on the same street, just a few buildings apart. This was a small relief—I wasn't too far from my mother, which was fortunate because things could have turned out even worse in St- Michel.

Around this time, my parents were searching for ways to improve their lives and patch up their marriage. They participated in a program called 'Marriage Encounter,' a weekend experience designed to help couples communicate more intimately. But it didn't seem to help much, as my father was increasingly absent. After that, they enrolled in another self-improvement program called EST Training (Erhard Seminar Training), now known as Landmark. This controversial program, notorious for its physically and emotionally demanding nature, spanned two weekends and aimed to help participants confront their issues and break free from their recurring negative patterns.

Even after that, I didn't notice any major changes in my parents, except that my mother seemed more assertive. That summer, for instance, when I knocked on her door, telling her that Dad hadn't come home for three days and that our fridge was empty, she refused to let me in. She stood behind the screen door and said, "I'm already responsible for five kids. Your father needs to step up and take care of you and your brothers." She knew full well he wasn't around much, but that day, she drew her line. That day, I walked back home with an empty stomach, realizing that my brothers—aged twelve and thirteen—and I would have to fend for ourselves in my father's absence.

Personally, I sometimes got invited to Sylvio's house for dinner. His father, a man in his late thirties living on welfare, welcomed me with open arms and would even offer me homemade cigarettes rolled from tobacco scraps he collected at bus stops. But that wasn't every day, and I couldn't rely on him for my survival. So, soon, my brothers and I started searching for ways to make money. At first, we collected empty refundable bottles, rummaging through trash bins. But soon, we began sneaking into backyards and climbing balconies to steal empty beer containers. One evening, as I was coming down the stairs of a building, I found a pair of jeans hanging on a clothesline. Since I barely had any clothes, I took them. Another night, I found a nearly new sweater. Eventually, we started bringing home bottles of chocolate milk and cream that we stole from a milkman's truck parked behind his house. He had a bad habit of leaving the truck unlocked. We made homemade butter with the cream and spread it on the few slices of bread we had in the fridge.

We went back to that truck a few times, but one evening, the milkman caught us. He'd been keeping watch from his window and chased us onto his balcony. I was terrified and ran faster than I ever had in my life. My brothers and I managed to escape, and we never went back.

Despite that scare, we continued our nightly escapades. In December of that same year, we stumbled upon a delivery truck full of cakes. The back door was easy to open, so we broke in and grabbed a dozen cakes to take home. That small heist made our Christmas a little sweeter; even without gifts or a tree in the house, since my father was still nowhere to be found.

Primary School

I remember attending St. Noel Chabanel Primary School for my fourth grade and for the first day of my fifth. However, most of my memories from school during those years and the previous ones are hazy. Just fragments remain. I remember Madam LeBeau, who used to tell me to stop yawning like a crow. Or that other lady who I thought was really nice and who I wished was my mother. I also recall a fight with a much smaller guy who still managed to beat me up. And my friendship with Sylvio, a kid from the building next door who lived with his father, whom I tried to convince that the bag of parsley I brought to school was weed. We would become very good friends, for a little while.

From the very first hour of class, when I returned to 5th grade, my name, Laflèche, would once again ruin my life. That morning, the teacher, who had seated me in the front row, asked each of us to stand and briefly introduce ourselves. Dreading the moment I'd have to say my name in front of the class, I quickly stood and spoke when it was my turn. Surprised to hear me say, "*Laflèche*," the teacher interrupted, "*I didn't ask for your last name, just your first name.*" My face turned red as I assured her that Laflèche was indeed my first name. She stared at me, incredulous, pretending not to understand. Her reaction, combined with the giggles from the class, felt like a personal attack. Angry and humiliated, I snapped back at her and was promptly sent to the principal's office.

Frustrated, I got up and made my way toward the door. At that moment, one of my classmates made a snide remark that set me off. Determined not to let it slide, I pulled a box of matches from my pocket— I had recently started smoking—and threw one at his hair. Naturally, the teacher demanded I hand over the matches. Already bruised by embarrassment, I refused and stormed out of the classroom, running to hide in the school's basement near the boiler room. This only escalated things, and the school administration immediately sent me home. It turned out to be my last day of school that year, as I flat-out refused to return. Surprisingly, my parents didn't seem too concerned. Maybe they believed, as followers of the faith, that since I was born consecrated in The Mission, I already had all the knowledge I needed, instilled by the 'Light' that had enlightened and instructed me even before birth! Perhaps that's what they told themselves, avoiding any serious efforts to ensure I went back to school.

Surrogate Father

After that day, I began spending a lot of time on my own, either staying at home or wandering around the neighborhood. I occasionally chatted with Sylvio's father when he came out on his balcony. He was kind and assured my father that I was always welcome at his place. He offered to keep an eye on me and make sure I had something to eat. Since he was already looking after his son, it was no trouble for him. When he learned I wasn't attending school, he even suggested that I join him in the afternoons so I wouldn't be alone. We could wait together for Sylvio to return from school. Eventually, I decided to stay there, since I could watch television and smoke cigarettes.

However, one afternoon, he took me to his room and sexually assaulted me. I was completely unprepared for that. At that moment, overwhelmed and frightened by what was happening, I remained motionless, unsure of what was occurring or what would come next. As he climbed on top of me, I felt a terrifying sense of detachment, as if I were leaving my body. I observed the scene from a distance, letting him do as he wished, fearing that resistance might provoke violence. It was only recently that I learned that detachment, a form of psychological protection, is known as dissociation. Terrified and unable to confront the reality of the situation, I retreated into this state as a defense mechanism.

"If you dissociate, you may feel disconnected from yourself and the world around you. For instance, you might feel detached from your body or as if the world around you is unreal. Remember, everyone's experience of dissociation is different. It's one way the mind copes with excessive stress, such as during a traumatic event." [14]

Frozen with fear, I remained motionless as Sylvio's father did what he wanted, his large, bright eyes staring at me with an almost otherworldly intensity. He kept insisting that I was an angel who had come down from heaven just for him. His words both surprised and confused me; this man seemed crazy. Yet, his description of me as an 'angel' reassured me a little. If I was an angel, surely, he wouldn't harm me and would eventually let me go. Secured by this idea, I instinctively stayed silent, hoping he would finish quickly.

When he was done, he instructed me to remain silent. He promised that as long as I did, everything would be fine, and I could return to eat, smoke cigarettes, and watch cable television with him and Sylvio— something I did that day and every day after. I grew accustomed to living with an overwhelming sense of shame. Overwhelmed, I began to isolate myself from the world, trying to push away the swirling thoughts in my head: What would my father say if he knew? What about my siblings—would they call me a fag? Was I? Was what happened to me okay? So many questions that I learned to ignore. The shame I felt from that day transformed into a sense of helplessness. It was just the way things were, and I couldn't change what had happened—I had to accept it. At the tender age of ten, I told myself that these abuses weren't so bad, as they provided me with security and attention in return.

For a while, I continued to hang out with my friend Sylvio, but slowly, a distance grew between us, and our friendship ended. One night, while I was staying over at his place, his father invaded my privacy again. That evening, Sylvio and I were chatting in his bed, unable to sleep. When we heard his father coming to turn off the light, we closed our eyes, pretending to be asleep. Thinking he was the only one awake, Sylvio's father leaned over me, kissed me, and whispered things in my ear before leaving without even saying goodnight to his son. I had trouble falling asleep that night. In the following days, I suspected Sylvio knew but was unwilling to talk about it. From that moment on, things were never the same between us. Despite this, I spent Christmas with him and his father, as we had no plans at home. My father was absent, and my mother was either too busy with my siblings or too depressed to insist I stay with them for Christmas.

However, this would be my last visit to his house. That evening, after our holiday meal, the three of us went to my mother to ask if I could join them for midnight mass at the local Catholic church. When she saw Sylvio's father standing beside me, she firmly refused and ordered me to return home. The next day, she lectured me and forbade me from going back to this man's house.

To this day, I wonder why my mother reacted so strongly. Was it because this man insisted on taking me to the "dwelling place of Satan," or had she sensed that he was a predator? Regardless, she seemed to regain her senses. In the following days, she allowed me back into the house, probably knowing I was too often alone. However, she insisted I make myself useful by helping her prepare dinner since I wasn't attending school.

Around that time, one of my father's cousins, who was fifteen, came to live with us. He had fled his home after his father, a staunch adherent of The Mission, threatened him with a wrench. I liked him, even though he took over my father's bedroom—the room I used when he was working nights. Because of this, I ended up sleeping in the living room.

However, his presence, along with that of his brother, who occasionally visited, was comforting. I felt less under the influence of my brothers, who had taken it upon themselves to "educate" me in place of my parents. Both were karate enthusiasts and brought some much-needed action into our lives. Meeting others who had also left The Mission confirmed that we weren't the only ones breaking away from the cult. It felt as though we were forming a new clan, no longer entirely alone in our exile from our former community. The presence of these other consecrated children, now considered children of Satan, filled a small part of the void left by our departure from The Mission. To this day, I still wonder what sin my father's cousin might have committed to force him to flee his father.

"In The Mission, it was like that! It was up to parents to ensure that children stayed on track and didn't behave like people of the world by doing evil. No matter what means we used, it was essential! They had to be corrected. It was for their own good." — Comment collected from a former mother of The Mission.

My Summer in a Commune

To keep the family united, my parents sometimes organized activities for all of us. At the start of summer, they took us for a day in the countryside to a commune run by a dozen hippies who practiced nudism. Located in the lower Laurentians in Quebec, it was a charming place frequented by one of my father's friends. I instantly loved it and quickly made friends with other children my age. Noticing how happy and engaged I was, my parents arranged for me to stay there for a few days under the care of a kind gentleman named Bernard. He gave me attention without asking for anything in return. Being there was incredible. It shifted my perspective on life, seeing people live with such freedom, close to nature, eating food from their gardens, and swimming in the lake. I ended up spending the entire summer there, surrounded by nature and good company. In that place, the hippies smoked constantly, so I began doing like them. Picking up a discarded joint from the ground or an ashtray and taking a few puffs became routine for me. That summer, I saw more shooting stars and auroras than I would for the rest of my life. When the season ended, I returned to Montreal with cherished memories and a new habit of smoking grass.

CHAPTER 7

FROM THE MISSION TO SCIENTOLOGY

One morning in 1983, my father, who had been growing increasingly absent since our departure from The Mission, reappeared, beaming with joy. It was reassuring to see him so lighthearted and carefree, as if everything would be all right from now on. He excitedly announced that he had joined a new movement, a "religious philosophy," as he called it. He had found Scientology. He was probably introduced to it by his friend Michel-Georges, by someone he met on a movie set where he was working at that time, or perhaps through EST Training. But it didn't matter; all that counted was that my father seemed to have found hope again. Scientology would become his new religion, and L. Ron Hubbard, its founder, became his new guru.

Hubbard, an American fiction writer, and master hypnotist born on March 13, 1911, in Tilden, Nebraska, had first ventured into parapsychology by proposing a therapeutic technique that, according to Jon Atack in Let's Sell These People a Piece of Blue Sky, was "strongly inspired" by Joseph Breuer's original therapeutic method, which Freud had rejected for fostering too much dependence on the therapist. In 1950, he published a "practical manual," Dianetics, claiming he had written it in just three weeks. He presented it as "The Modern Science of Mental Health." In it, Hubbard proposed a new therapeutic technique that he asserted performed miracles.

Published shortly after World War II, during the onset of the Cold War, Dianetics was touted as "The only mental science capable of ridding Man of all madness and aberration" by eliminating the reactive mind and making one a 'Clear'— as in cleared from his reactive mind. According to Hubbard, this technique could create a superior 'race,' not through eugenics but through therapy. Despite its early hype, the book's initial glory quickly faded.

At the Church of Scientology on Boulevard Papineau in Montreal, they didn't inform my father that several experts had denounced the theories and practices of the book in the year Dianetics was published.

"For most doctors, the concept known as Dianetics is neither scientific nor worthy of discussion or revision." [15]

As soon as the book Dianetics was published, the American Psychological Association condemned the technique in an article in the New York Times, highlighting its dangers.[16] The following year, Dr. Joseph Augustus Winter, who had previously been associated with Hubbard, published another book[17] vigorously denouncing Dianetics. This book featured an introduction by German psychiatrist Frederick Perls, a specialist in Gestalt Therapy. Dianetics also faced criticism from the American Psychiatric Society. It was from this failure that Scientology emerged. With his exceptional charisma and vivid imagination, Hubbard convinced the Dianeticists gathered at his Dianetic Foundation that he had transformed his technology into something more practical and miraculous. He knew some people were willing to sacrifice everything to reach higher levels of existence. Seizing on this, he offered them a path to Total Freedom, exploiting the extraordinary 'human potential' they represented for his own ends.

From his science fiction writer's office, Hubbard took to the pulpit, organizing conference after conference, promising anyone who would listen that he could elevate a man to god-like status, just as Eugène Richer had claimed to do before him. Thanks to his many followers, Hubbard quickly spread Scientology across the United States. Within a few years of his first conference, around ten churches had sprung up in various states. Hubbard attracted thousands of followers, contributing to the growth of Scientology as a popular religion. Unlike traditional religions that promised paradise, Scientology offered powers previously thought unattainable here on earth.

My father probably saw in Scientology a project similar to the one proposed by The Mission, which aimed to recreate godlike individuals. Not through ecumenism this time, but with therapy.

Scientology: Religion for Profit?

From 1958, four years after Scientology's inception, the religious status of Hubbard's churches faced scrutiny from American tax authorities. Scientology lost its tax-exempt status when it was revealed that, over four years, Hubbard had spent more than $100,000 of the Church's funds on personal needs. The following year, he attempted to establish himself in Great Britain, but from the early 1960s, Scientology became a subject of controversy across the Anglo-Saxon world. Amid growing concerns and numerous complaints, several governments launched investigation commissions to uncover the true nature of the New Religious Movement—NRM. In 1965, the "Anderson Report," commissioned by the State of Victoria in Australia, concluded with these words:

"Scientology is evil; its techniques are evil. Its practice poses a serious threat to the community on medical, moral, and social levels, as well as to its adherents, who are sadly deceived and often mentally ill... The Commission found nothing of value for the community in Scientology." [18]

The release of this report prompted the Victorian state government to impose strict regulations on psychological practices and related fields, leading to Scientology's ban in several Australian states. Alongside this, Hubbard, his supporters, and Scientology faced bans in other Anglo-Saxon countries, including the United Kingdom, South Africa, and New Zealand. Hubbard was also barred from Rhodesia (now Zimbabwe). In 1967, he even relocated to a ship operating in international waters to evade legal action. In 1970, the Lee Report in Ontario, Canada, did not call for a ban on Scientology in the province but recommended close monitoring of its activities:

"Scientology should not be excluded from the proscriptions of the practice of medicine under the Medical Act on the grounds of being a religion." [19]

Around the same time, a British House of Commons report criticized Scientology's psychotherapeutic methods, deeming them a menace to public and individual health. As a result, British authorities barred foreign Scientologists from accessing the advanced organization at Saint Hill in Sussex. [20]

In 1970, journalist George Malko published a critical book titled "Scientology, The Now Religion." The following year, ex-Scientologist Cyril Vosper released "The Mind Benders," the first critical book by a former Scientologist.

In 1971, American journalist Paulette Cooper also published "The Scandal of Scientology."

In 1972, Ron DeWolf, the founder's eldest son, participated in the promotion of "Inside Scientology" by former Scientologist Robert Kaufman, which sharply criticized Scientology and its founder.

In 1977, during raids on Scientology premises, the FBI uncovered documents detailing strategies to neutralize American authorities. These criminal operations, in the 1970s, named Operation Snow White, aimed to purge files unfavorable to Scientology from targeted offices. Thousands of Scientology members executed a series of infiltrations and thefts in 136 government agencies, foreign embassies, consulates, and private organizations critical of Scientology across more than thirty countries.

Following the 1978 trial, American and Canadian courts indicted eleven high-ranking Church officials, including Mary Sue Hubbard, the founder's wife and chief operative in the infiltration scheme. Some pleaded guilty, while others were convicted by the Federal Court for obstruction of justice, theft of documents and state property, and burglary of government offices. They received prison terms of four to five years and fines of $10,000.

Hubbard was labeled a 'co-conspirator' by the federal prosecutor but was not prosecuted, likely due to his collaborators taking the fall and the lack of a direct link between him and the crimes. However, his wife, Mary Sue, was sentenced to five years in prison and recognized as the principal leader of Operation Snow White. The FBI raid also enabled American authorities to seize nearly 50,000 documents and other evidence related to various operations conducted by Hubbard's intelligence agency, the Guardian Office, later renamed the Office of Special Affairs.

This organization aimed to infiltrate government offices in multiple countries. Operations such as "Freak Out," "Daniel," and "Dynamite" were designed to neutralize journalist Paulette Cooper by attempting to charge her falsely with crimes or commit her to a psychiatric institution. In 1978, French authorities convicted L. Ron Hubbard in absentia for fraud. He was sentenced to a fine of $35,000 and four years in prison, a sentence he never served.

Dad Discovers Scientology

In this new religious movement, my father was likely offered solutions to his problems through various personal improvement courses designed for newcomers to the church. He must have been introduced to the "Bridge to Total Freedom," a series of stages that would elevate a being— referred to as a 'Thetan'—to higher levels of existence, such as the state of 'Clear' and the levels known as Operating Thetan[21], or OTs.

In 1983, my father innocently walked into a Scientology church with several members of our family, including my seven siblings and me. At the same time, a custody trial was unfolding across the Atlantic. A mother of two, an ex-Scientologist, was fighting for full custody of her children from their father, who remained a Scientologist. During the hearings, Hubbard's true nature was exposed.

The founder of Scientology falsely presented himself in the literature of his 'Church' as a highly decorated war hero of the American Navy. However, his Navy service records reveal that his military performances were substandard. He briefly commanded two small anti-submarine vessels in coastal waters but was removed from command of both. His superiors rated him as unsuitable for independent duties. Hubbard was awarded only a few campaign medals and was never given the Purple Heart medal he claimed to have received. He also fabricated his academic credentials, misleading everyone into believing he held a degree in nuclear physics. [22]

In the custody verdict, where custody was awarded to the ex-Scientologist mother, the judge remarked:

"Scientology is both immoral and socially obnoxious... In my judgment, it is corrupt, sinister, and dangerous. It is corrupt because it is based on lies and deceit and has as its real objective money and power for Mr. Hubbard, his wife, and those close to him at the top. It is sinister because it indulges in infamous practices both to its adherents who do not toe the line unquestioningly and to those who criticize or oppose it. It is dangerous because it is out to capture people, especially children and impressionable young people, and indoctrinate and brainwash them so that they become the unquestioning captives and tools for the cult, withdrawn from ordinary thought, living, and relationship with others." [23]

Since then, more than twenty judges worldwide have condemned Scientology in trials for fraud, harassment, theft, and more. Additionally, plenty of people have denounced this NRM through books, television interviews, or articles. Back in 1983, when our family joined Scientology, Hubbard, by then nearly senile, was holed up in a motorhome stationed somewhere in Southern California, near the headquarters of the organization managing its international churches. He continued to hide to avoid personal accountability for the multitude of lawsuits against him and his New Religious Movement and still drew significant financial benefits from his churches, which were registered as charities. [24]

I would only discover the truth about this man after spending several years in this 'science of mind distortion,' called Scientology, dedicating time and money to it because I believed in Hubbard and his New Religious Movement.

CHAPTER 8

WHEN MISFORTUNE OF SOME MAKES THE FORTUNE OF OTHERS

Although, on the surface, Scientology may not have seemed to share much with the Mission of the Holy Spirit, my father found several similarities between the two new religious movements that drew his adherence:

An infallible guru;
The belief that man is a spiritual being who reincarnates life after life, carrying 'baggage' with him;
A method to improve the intelligence and psyche of individuals;
A plan for the rescue and regeneration of humanity
The observation that humanity is heading toward its doom;
The idea that children should have maximum autonomy.

"In Scientology, self-determination is indeed described as a state where an individual can choose whether or not to be controlled by their environment. This concept emphasizes having confidence in one's ability to control the physical universe and manage various aspects of life. [...] The child has the right to self-determination." [25]

Hubbard portrayed children as million-year-old beings:

"A child is not a special kind of animal different from Man. A child is a man or a woman who has not attained full growth." [26]

"The sweetness and love of a child will continue as long as he can have his own self-determinism. If you interfere with his self-determinism, you are interfering with his life." [27]

This kind of discourse justified my father's behavior over the years. It gave him confidence that we could manage our lives "independently." Over the next thirty years, he would donate more than $300,000 to the Church of Scientology, most of it earned as a cab driver, while we, his wife and children, lived in poverty. He also found a new target for his hatred: psychiatry and psychology. Hubbard labeled all psychologists and psychiatrists as dangers to humanity. In The Mission, my father had already been encouraged to oppose "false theories whose application would bring catastrophes... systems tinged with 'Freudism.'"[28] Like his new guru, my father became fiercely opposed to psychology and psychiatry.

Hubbard and psychiatrist

Why did Hubbard loathe 'shrinks' so much? First, since he presented Scientology as a new mental science, it gave him an advantage to suggest that these fields were outdated, barbaric, and harmful. Furthermore, psychologists have thoroughly criticized his Dianetics and Scientology. Hubbard's aversion can also be understood in light of research by his critics, such as Russell Miller,[29] who mentions in his book Bare-Faced Messiah, that Hubbard's divorce from his second wife, Sarah Hollister, whom he beat, just like Eugène Richer dit Laflèche did with his wife:

Sarah accused her husband of frequently trying to strangle her; on one occasion, shortly before Christmas 1950, he had been so violent he ruptured the Eustachian tube in her left ear. (...) the divorce complaint continued, the 'plaintiff and her medical advisers... concluded that said Hubbard was hopelessly insane, and crazy, and that there was no hope for said Hubbard, any reason for her to endure further; that said "Hubbard be committed to a private sanatorium for psychiatric observation and treatment of a mental ailment known as paranoid schizophrenia...". [30]

Shortly after my father encountered Scientology, my parents reconciled, and we moved into a large apartment near the Church of Scientology in Montreal, on Le Plateau-Mont-Royal. Before we had even settled in, Dad introduced us to Scientology. One of my older brothers joined the staff as soon as we arrived in the neighborhood. As for me, moving from Saint-Michel allowed me to escape the predator who had abused me the previous year. However, it also meant I was off the Director of Youth Protection's radar, who might have helped me find someone to talk to about my aversion to school and secured my eventual return. But my parents didn't seem to mind my absence from school, nor did they seek help from professionals, probably convinced to keep me away from the 'psych' by Hubbard's teachings propagated by Scientology churches:

"The reason people started to confuse children with dogs and started training children with force lies in the field of psychology. The psychologist worked on 'principles' as follows:
Man is evil.
Man must be trained into being a social animal.
Man must adapt to his environment.
As these postulates are false, psychology doesn't work. And if you ever saw a wreck, it's the child of a professional psychologist." [31]

To show Scientologists what the 'psychs' represented to him, Hubbard published Battlefield Earth in 1982. In this science fiction novel, a race of monstrous aliens called 'Psychlos' occupies Earth, which they invaded a thousand years ago. By using the prefix 'psych' for these invaders, Hubbard implied they were akin to psychiatrists. He used this strategy to dehumanize every professional whose title starts with the prefix 'psych.' As a child, I was easily swayed by such a maneuver!

The Plateau-Mont-Royal

One of the very few positive aspects of Scientology was that its Montreal headquarters was located on the Plateau Mont-Royal. I had fallen in love with that borough of Montreal from the moment we moved there, in 1983. Back then, the area offered much lower rent and a more diverse population than it does today, with people from all walks of life. Artistic institutions, including the Conservatory of Music of Montreal, the National Theater School of Canada, the Grands Ballets Canadiens, UQAM (University of Quebec in Montreal), and several theaters such as Le Rideau Vert, Le Théâtre de Quat'Sous, La Licorne, and Le Théâtre d'Aujourd'hui.

In my first week on the Plateau, I ran into a friend from the hippie commune I had visited the previous year. Dressed as a clown, she was selling helium balloons in Lafontaine Park with her student friends from UQAM. She introduced me to this group of young artists, who quickly became very dear to me. I resonated with their 'way of life,' reminiscent of the people I had met in the commune the summer before. I met François, a multidisciplinary artist who lived with his girlfriend, who lent me the first novel I ever read: "The Hobbit" by Tolkien. There was also Bernard, the friendly painter who shared François' apartment, and Valerie, who I secretly fell for when she sang for me with her guitar. Another girl I liked, named Julie, had a roommate whose name escapes me—a punk who pierced my ear with an ice cube and a sewing needle one Sunday afternoon. An act that did not sit well with my parents when I returned home.

There was also Yves, the juggler, who lived in the building next door to where my family and I resided, just behind the Church of Scientology of Montreal, who was an outspoken critic of Scientology. I appreciated them all, especially because they were artists. They helped create the new environment I found myself in on the Plateau, which was a stark contrast to the one I had left in Saint-Michel. For the first time in a long while, I felt truly happy, much like I had with my hippie friends the previous summer.

I spent a lot of time with them from the moment I arrived on the Plateau Mont-Royal at eleven, while they were all nineteen or twenty. I felt privileged, and even today, I look back on that period of my life with deep nostalgia. I often dream of reconnecting with those friends who abruptly vanished from my life in the week following my twelfth birthday. That day, I visited François, who lived on Mont-Royal Street, just a few steps from our home and the Church of Scientology. Cheerful, I mentioned that I was celebrating my birthday. He asked how old I was, and I truthfully replied that I had just turned twelve. The shock on his face was palpable when he realized I was much younger than he had assumed, as I looked fourteen or fifteen and smoked and drank alcohol. From that day forward, my friends gradually stopped 'opening their doors to me.' They probably felt I should spend time with peers my own age rather than in their world of young university students, where sex, drugs, and alcohol were prevalent.

Today, I remain nostalgic for that time, which marked a significant turning point in my life. I doubt my old artist friends will ever fully understand how their sudden absence impacted me, steering my life in a direction far removed from the path I was on with them, who had not fallen into Scientology's trap.

CHAPTER 9

BEGINNING OF MY STUDIES IN SCIENTOLOGY

*"Discipline in itself is not a poisonous concept.
Only discipline imposed instead of being chosen is."*

Jack Vance

Since I didn't return to school in 1983, I had a lot of free time to fill. I tried to visit François a few times, but his door remained closed, and it seemed like all my other friends had vanished, too. So, I began spending more and more time at the Church of Scientology, where Dad had enrolled me in my first 'personal improvement' class. I liked the idea of studying in an environment where I was often the only child. It also pleased my parents, who preferred me in this classroom rather than roaming the streets and alleys of Montreal.

I officially began my Scientology training in the Basic Courses room, where newcomers take introductory courses before they sign up for major courses and are allowed to enter the larger academy for more advanced Scientology studies. On my first day, I met the supervisor responsible for ensuring that the study period ran smoothly. He explained that his role was not to teach but to make sure that everything in the room adhered to the guidelines set by Hubbard. He outlined the classroom rules: no food or drink allowed on the premises, no chatting between students, no tolerance for lateness, whether at the start of lessons or after breaks, and others. He also mentioned that leaving the classroom before a break to make a phone call or use the bathroom was strictly forbidden without prior permission. Such an action would be considered a harmful act called a 'blow,' which usually led to significant disciplinary consequences, starting with a visit to the ethics department. Scientologists are constantly monitored by their peers, course supervisors, or hierarchical superiors, particularly if they are staff members. A Scientologist must report any actions considered contrary to the group's policies, survival, image, or expansion through "Knowledge Reports," which are sent to the ethics department. This department carefully preserves these reports and addresses the situations that need attention.

Stuck on a chair

The first course I enrolled in, "The Basic Study Manual," contained rules deemed essential for success in studies by Hubbard, who claimed studying could be daunting. He provided us with 'tools' to succeed in our studies. I was skeptical about the need to "learn how to learn," given that I had always received good grades in school. For me, studying was an activity that allowed me to evolve, develop my intellect, and enrich my knowledge base. My lack of interest in school had nothing to do with studying itself, and I saw no need to learn a different method for it.

However, I soon realized that Scientology's approach to study was not about analysis or interpretation. We were not there to reflect but to quickly assimilate the concepts Hubbard presented without questioning them. These concepts were to be taken literally and duplicated exactly in our minds. The 'tools' provided in the course were mainly there to ensure that we integrated Scientology's new concepts correctly. Actually, I didn't feel I needed to learn how to learn, but I had to succeed in this compulsory course to be admitted to other Scientology courses.

One of the key concepts taught in this course was that skipping a misunderstood word in the text could make the entire sentence and subsequent paragraphs incomprehensible.

Encountering such a word would cause unpleasant symptoms in the student, which would be visible to the supervisor. For example, the student might appear exhausted, detached, or develop a sort of nervous hysteria, feeling inept about the subject matter. According to Hubbard, ignoring misunderstood words would also encourage the student to abandon their studies and leave the course without authorization, which was considered a 'blow.' I quickly learned to hide any sign of boredom or disinterest while studying Scientology. However, one day, I made the mistake of being candid with one of the course supervisors who hovered around me. I told him honestly that my disinterest stemmed from finding the teachings useless. My boredom was the only reason I was in a bad state and considered leaving.

The course supervisor insisted that my 'inability' to grasp the importance and validity of the text must be due to misunderstood words. Hubbard was adamant about this. As his role was to ensure I wasn't committing 'a crime' by failing to clarify these words, he withdrew me from the course and sent me directly to the ethics department. Hubbard was fond of the term 'crime' and established a parallel justice system and a department in each of his organizations to oversee it.

The Ethic Department

Thus, from my very first days in Scientology, I found myself facing the church's Ethics Officer, needing to explain my behavior. That member of the staff explained that his role in the organization was to ensure Scientology was applied correctly. Hubbard suggested that man is driven by a single impulse: survival, which makes life a constant challenge. According to the Ethics Officer, Hubbard was a genius who devised a straightforward system he called ethics conditions.
This system was meant to help individuals achieve optimal survival by applying a system elaborated to constantly improve one's conditions of existence. Regardless of an individual's 'survival level.'

The Ethics Officer also explained that certain areas of one's life, which he referred to as dynamics, involved other people and sometimes needed reinforcement by a senior member. In Montreal's Scientology organization, the Ethics Officer's job was to help improve the conditions of the group. To make sure its survival potential was not compromised. Since I had not followed the group classroom rules and had rebelled against Hubbard's authority and the supervisor, he had to use the ethics system to help me become a good participant. He assigned me a condition of 'danger,' which came with an ethics program to complete before returning to the course room.

To improve my condition as a group member, I had to apply Hubbard's formulas, which involved a series of steps that began by having to choose between analyzing and criticizing Hubbard's teachings or accepting to apply his 'technology' without making any comments. The Ethics Officer was to monitor my progress, ensuring I was not a threat to the group's survival and that I applied the ethics conditions formulas to restore my reputation with the group and with the course room supervisor.

One of the steps in these formulas was to ask other group members for permission to return among those who fully apply Hubbard's technology. I was also instructed to write down all the destructive actions" I had committed against the group and Hubbard, such as skipping over misunderstood words or criticizing Scientology's teachings. These writings would be recorded in an ethics file that he would keep indefinitely.

The process felt overwhelming, but since I wanted to improve my survival skills, I agreed to submit to the program. At eleven, I couldn't fully analyze it and did not understand that I was asked to ignore my thinking and conform to Hubbard's ideology. I just told myself that perhaps they had something better for me.

From then on, I saw myself as a full member of the group. I followed the rules, stopped doubting the founder of Scientology, and focused on 'duplicating' Hubbard's teachings while maintaining a smile and keeping my back straight to avoid further scrutiny. Looking for misunderstood words whenever I felt something was wrong with what I was reading. That way, I quickly completed the course and was allowed to sign up for the next one.

The Communication Course

The next class my father signed me up for was the Communication Course. It consisted mainly of practical exercises called TRs (Training Routines), which were designed to enhance my ability to communicate with others. There again, I felt I even had less need to learn how to communicate than to learn how to study. I had never struggled with socializing. However, my father assured me that this course would be highly beneficial for me. And since that course was recommended to almost every newcomer, I didn't argue and followed the registrar's directives.

The TRs were presented as exercises aimed at improving one's control over communication—an essential skill for Scientology therapists who needed to support their clients through challenging sessions. However, they were initially introduced by Hubbard as therapeutic processes in the Scientology therapy catalog in 1957. Only later were they offered to the public as part of the Communication Course. Hubbard concealed these potent processes within these communication exercises. I would experience their effects while performing what I believed were simple communication drills.

For the TRs practice, I faced another student seated about a meter away from me. I had to sit upright, hands on my thighs, avoiding any movement, with my eyes closed. I remained in this posture for a relatively long time. It felt somewhat like meditation, though we never used that term in Scientology. Initially, I found it uncomfortable and struggled to 'abandon myself.' The presence of the other student felt intrusive, as though my privacy was being invaded. I only felt comfortable when I 'allowed' my twin student and the supervisor, who sometimes stood beside me, into my 'space.' I had to trust them while keeping my eyes closed to relax fully.

After a few hours of practice, I could sit still for about thirty minutes without moving and stay relaxed, a state of being I maintained for the rest of the day. With a serene demeanor, I received a 'pass' and was allowed to move on to the next exercise, TR 0 'Confrontation.'

The next Training Routine required me to be more alert. It was similar to the first one but performed with my eyes open, this time staring directly into the eyes of the other student. The TR began when one of us said, 'Start.' From that moment, I could not look away, close my eyes, or move. Any movement of my hand, leg, lips, foot, or any part of my body resulted in a 'flunk,' and I had to restart the exercise. Showing any emotions— sighing in weariness, laughing at random thoughts, or even reacting to the situation—was also prohibited. We had to remain still, even if our posture caused leg or back pain.

I found this exercise painful. My eyes often burned, and I had to suppress many yawns. The supervisor occasionally gave the starting signal and decided when to end the practice of this 'communication exercise.' I could not leave the course voluntarily for a break or to look outside. Leaving without authorization was considered a 'blow,' so I had no choice but to comply and stay until the end of the period.

TR 0 'Confrontation' was presented as a means to improve an auditor's (Scientology counselor) ability to 'stand firm' and maintain the communication cycle even if the person in therapy became agitated or aggressive. With this in mind, I practiced TR 0, accepting what lay ahead without question.

Hypnotic Induction

"Hypnotic induction is an essential prerequisite for achieving hypnosis itself. Its objective is to channel the subject's attention to trigger the state of dissociation. The subject must remain lucid and aware of what is happening around him while taking a certain distance from it. To achieve this goal, the hypnotherapist uses different techniques to exclusively stimulate one of the patient's sensory channels, such as sight." [32]

Practicing this TR was tough on my back, buttocks, and neck, with pains that had begun during the previous TR when my eyes were closed. Adding to that, the strain of staring into my twin's eyes for extended periods felt almost like torture. However, I made sure not to comment on Hubbard's methods and persevered despite the increasing discomfort. I had to endure. The manual claimed that all symptoms during the exercise would vanish with persistence, so I pushed through, trying to ignore the pain and the absurdity of it all. I remember feeling disoriented while practicing, but I convinced myself it would make me tougher, so I challenged myself to succeed, even when my instincts and judgment urged me to stop.

Then came the symptoms described in the book. After several hours of struggling, my suffering became so intense that I let myself detach from it. My vision blurred, and a gray cloud seemed to appear between me and the student in front of me. His features distorted as if he were made of rubber and had been struck on the head. At that moment, I felt a detachment from my painful body. The suffering became more manageable and easier to endure. As though I had entered a new 'state of being' in which the physical universe became secondary. Within a few days of practicing TR 0 'Confrontation,' I quickly found this new distant state I had discovered and could remain in it for extended periods. The exercise became easy, and I was allowed to move on to the next one.

The difficulty of the TRs gradually increased, and moral harassment was now incorporated alongside the challenge of the exercises. In the next stage, I had to remain seated and maintain the detached state achieved in previous exercises while my twin verbally provoked me, trying to disorient me and make me lose control.He sought sensitive points to press, using provocations, humiliation, or playful teasing—making faces or agitating his body. Initially, I enjoyed TR 0 'Bull Bait' until my twin discovered my sensitive spots. Comments like, "You look like a little girl with your long hair!" or "I saw you looking at that boy's butt!" triggered reactions from me, which my twin noted with 'flunks.' He continued to exploit these triggers and found new ones. I had to train myself to remain unresponsive and stay disconnected from my emotions.

After several practice sessions, I was able to maintain my 'serenity' regardless of his attempts, no longer letting his words or actions affect me. I then received a new 'pass.'

"Dissociation is a break in how your mind handles information. You may feel disconnected from your thoughts, feelings, memories, and surroundings. It can affect your sense of identity and your perception of time." [33]

It felt great to be in that state where I could retreat instantly. I continued practicing exercises from the Communication Course, working on controlling communication while in that dissociated state. At a certain point, I would slip into this slight hypnotic trance state every time I entered a Scientology organization! In fact, it became almost permanent for me.

"Some cults incorporate mind-numbing or mind-altering practices into their one-on-one or group gatherings to put individuals in a trance-like state, making them more easily influenced and controlled, and more susceptible to stealth suggestions."

Bonnie Zieman[34]

CHAPTER 10

SCIENTOLOGY

PSEUDOSCIENCE OF KNOWLEDGE

"In hypnosis terms, suggestions are statements made with the intention of influencing someone's mindset. The hypnotist uses suggestions to alter the way a client thinks about something, change their feelings towards something, or inspire positive emotions."³ ⁴Hippolyte Bernheim°35

According to Hippolyte Bernheim,[35] suggestion refers to the act of conveying a guiding idea through verbal or non-verbal language. While working within the Scientology organization in Montreal, I constantly saw posters plastered on the walls. Some were benign, announcing upcoming events or new courses and books. Others, however, displayed charts, codes, and scales illustrating the principles and concepts introduced by Hubbard. Since Scientology was presented as a science of the mind, these charts were prominently featured in classrooms and offices throughout the organization. Amongst many others, we found:

The Gradation Chart;
The Scientology Creed;
The Emotional Tone Scale.

The Gradation Chart is a poster outlining the steps to traverse the famous Bridge to Total Freedom, which my father was first introduced to upon joining Scientology. It consists of a series of steps leading to the state of Clear[36] and then to the state of OT[37] (Operating Thetan). Scientologists begin their journey at the bottom of the Bridge, progressing through Scientology therapies known as auditing processes.

The chart details the various states of consciousness and control over the universe one is expected to achieve through auditing, ranging from "The ability to communicate freely with anyone, on any subject" or "The ability to recognize and eliminate the source of our problems" at the lower levels, to "The ability to resolve the main causes of amnesia in all our past lives" at the highest levels. Naturally, I was skeptical when I read Hubbard's claim that reaching the top of the Bridge would allow a person to remember their numerous past lives. It seemed implausible. Yet, after experiencing profound detachment from my emotions while practicing the TRs, my opinion of Hubbard was elevated. This man had already managed to place me on a pink cloud, so I had begun to entertain the possibility that he might have made other significant discoveries like those he claimed. Perhaps he had found the key to total freedom from the physical universe.

The Creed of the Church of Scientology

Another poster in the Church's entrance hall was titled "The Creed of the Church of Scientology," outlining a set of principles proposed by Hubbard for Scientologists to follow in guiding their behavior. Each time I entered the building and passed by this poster, I would stop momentarily to read it.

"We of the Church believe: [...] That all men have the inalienable right to their own religious practices and their performance [...] That all men have the inalienable right to conceive, choose, assist, or support their own organizations, churches, and governments [...]"

The Creed began with these words, which seemed legitimate to me. However, as I read further down, the implications became clearer. Hubbard suggested that if I was experiencing mental illness, I should seek help from a church.

"That the study of the mind and the healing of mental illnesses should not be separated from religion, nor tolerated in non-religious fields."

According to this principle, modern medicine would be misguided in its approach, prioritizing the physical treatment of illnesses.

"And we of the Church believe that the spirit can be saved. And that the spirit alone may save or heal the body."

I saw this poster almost every day; Hubbard's principles embedded themselves in my mind, influencing my choices and actions even long after I stopped identifying as a Scientologist. Another poster that constantly drew my attention was the Tone Scale. I was fascinated by its small drawings depicting thetans at various emotional levels, including one illustrating the tone of a thetan without a body.

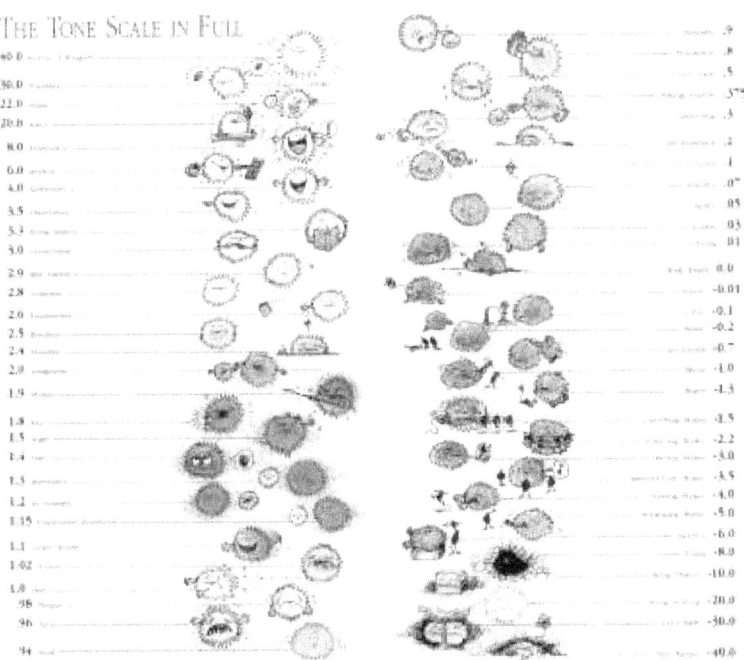

According to Hubbard, this scale was designed to evaluate people's emotional tone. At the top is tone 40, representing 'Serenity of Being,' with a smiling and satisfied thetan—the ideal state sought by Scientologists.

At the center of the scale, 0 represents the 'Death of the Body.' Below 0 are the emotional tones an aberrated, body-less thetan might experience. At twelve, I examined this poster with a mix of fascination and skepticism. Hubbard claimed, as the emojis show, that as we moved up the scale toward the summit, we approached ultimate survival and happiness. However, the progression of tones as written beside the drawing seemed contrary to my understanding of spirituality.

How could 'No Compassion' be at 1.2 while 'Compassion' was lower, at 0.9, dangerously close to 'Death of the Body' at 0.0? It suggested that a compassionate being was further from 'Serenity of Being' than someone with 'no compassion.'

Similarly, the scale placed 'Hate' at 1.4, 'Anger' at 1.5, 'Hostility' at 1.9, and 'Antagonism' at 2.0. According to Hubbard, these states were preferable to having 'Compassion' at 0.9 or seeking to 'Redeem' at 0.37. This seemed nonsensical to me, and despite my young age, it conflicted with my innate values.

Another puzzling aspect was 'Resentment' at 1.3 compared to 'Unexpressed Resentment' at 1.15. It implied that expressing your resentment was closer to the top than being tolerant. Again, I disagreed with Hubbard but kept my thoughts to myself; discussing them with the wrong person could lead to a visit to the ethics department.

Drastic Change in Attitude

Faced with so many contradictions, I eventually began to question my doubts about the Tone scale. I started to embrace Hubbard's ideology, convinced that this man, with extraordinary knowledge, who deserved to have a bust of him in the church hall, was of superior intelligence to mine. From then on, I aimed to remain at the top of the tone scale, avoiding the tonal zone below 2.0. I understood I had to adopt a new attitude and stay at the top of the Tone Scale, like other Scientologists. This was made easier by the dissociation generated through TRs, a modified state of consciousness that had become quasi-permanent.

"Today's programs are designed to destabilize an individual's sense of self by undermining his or her basic consciousness, reality, awareness, beliefs and worldview, emotional control and defense mechanism."
Margaret Thaler Singer, Cults in our Midst

I tried my best to forget my complicated past and stay at the top of the Tone scale around Exultation, Action, Games, Postulates, and Serenity of Being, even if it meant sacrificing my authenticity and ignoring my feelings. It was expected of me if I wanted to avoid rejection by my new Scientologist friends.

"It is not necessary to produce a world of clears to have a reasonable and worthwhile social order; it is only necessary to delete those individuals who range from 2.0 down, either by processing them enough to get their tone level above the 2.0 line—or simply quarantining them from society."
L. Ron Hubbard, Science of Survival.

Thus, I continued my education in Scientology, internalizing beliefs and values that I would later have to deprogram. In the Personal Integrity Course, I would learn a principle that would make leaving Scientology nearly impossible without experiencing shame or guilt. In that course, Hubbard suggested that the only reason an individual leaves a group without notice is that they have committed a crime and fear being discovered.

Sticking to this principle made it almost impossible for me to leave without being considered a criminal in the eyes of other Scientologists, including my father and family members who were in Scientology.

Oppression?

Another principle I learned in a beginner's course called 'The Ups and Downs in Life' (now The Cause of Suppression) influenced me long after leaving Scientology. Hubbard invented the concept of PTS/SP, which isolated Scientologists from those who opposed him and his Scientology. A PTS person—Potential Trouble Source—was considered a potential source of trouble, susceptible to illness, accidents, mistakes, mood swings, and so on, due to their relationship with an SP. The only reason a PTS would be in that state, according to Hubbard, is that this person is socially affected by a 'Suppressive Person' or 'antisocial personality.'

Hubbard claimed that 2.5% of people were true suppressive individuals, with another 20% having antisocial tendencies that could affect others.[38]

It meant that more than 22% of society might have an impact on those around them, which was a significant number of people to be wary of.

By Hubbard's policy, a Scientologist in contact with an SP could not study or receive Scientology procedures. When sick or considered PTS, they have to identify the person in their environment oppressing them before being allowed to return to their courses or auditing sessions. Most of the time, the SP found in the environment of the PTS is someone antagonistic to Scientology.

I learned to identify Suppressive Persons based on twelve criteria. The ninth characteristic, in particular, encouraged me to avoid those critical of Scientology, as it claimed to be dedicated to improving people and society.

"The antisocial personality supports only destructive groups and rages against and attacks any constructive or betterment group." [39]

Adhering to this principle made me highly judgmental, isolating me from many people. Scientology used this to keep me away from anyone who criticized Hubbard or Scientology by labeling them as SP.

This principle of PTS/SP led to real witch hunts and collateral damage. For instance, Danielle, a girl about my age whom I liked and enjoyed seeing at the Montreal Scientology organization, fell ill with leukemia and died. Her death was a tragic event for us, her friends, and undoubtedly for her mother, who not only lost her daughter but also faced cruel accusations from Scientologists. By adhering to Hubbard's teachings, Danielle was oppressed to the point of death by an SP. Some of us pointed out her mother for that.

CHAPTER 11

JOINING STAFF

From the age of twelve, I was permitted to sign a contract as a staff member at the Church of Scientology in Montreal. Since I was still required to attend school due to my age, I worked evenings and weekends. During the day, instead of attending classes, I roamed around, often knocking on François's door, which remained stubbornly closed. At night, I would either go to work or spend time in the course room since staff members were required to dedicate several hours each week to studying Hubbard's policies and strategies.

My shifts involved simple tasks: acting as a receptionist at the building's entrance, tidying up and cleaning spaces, filing bills in the treasury or central file, making postal deliveries, and handling other daily duties. I particularly enjoyed the team activities, like the large mailings that sometimes stretched late into the night. These tasks involved affixing stamps on envelopes and inserting advertisements, which were then sent to everyone who had provided their address to the organization when purchasing a book or taking a free personality test. Most of the time, there were hundreds of letters to be sent. On Saturdays and Sundays, I worked at the corner of Mont-Royal and Papineau for body-routing. This task involved approaching strangers on the street to invite them to take a free personality test, aiming to recruit new members. I learned to approach those who seemed friendly, engage them in conversation, and 'take control' by gently guiding them toward the Church. Initially, I was uncomfortable with the idea of controlling people and directing them toward the front door, but I was told it was for their own benefit.

My seniors referred to it as 'good control,' making me believe that by leading people to Hubbard's teachings, I was helping them and society, as some would end up buying a book or signing up for a course. I used to enjoy recruiting on the street until a few passersby, who were aware of Scientology and held a negative view of it, reprimanded me. Some even labeled it a cult. I didn't fully understand what that meant at the time, but I sensed it wasn't positive. After several negative encounters, I tried to avoid being assigned this task whenever possible.

Since I was in the building hosting the organization in the evenings, I occasionally served as the night watchman until an executive realized I was too young for the role. I felt insulted when I was told I could not do that job anymore because I was used to being treated like an adult. I liked working at night because it allowed me to explore the organization freely. I often sat in the large armchair in Hubbard's luxurious office—a space each organization had to maintain in case the founder decided to visit. Seeing the massive wooden library and the golden pen holder on the majestic oak desk, it was clear that Hubbard had high standards. I sometimes wondered why this office and its contents weren't made available to staff members who could have put them to good use. However, the office was strictly reserved for him, even though we all knew that the founder of Scientology would never actually visit the Church in Montreal.

Learning the Rules

Alongside my work, I underwent training through a course called 'Staff Status One,' which covered the many policies we had to follow as staff members. One of the first rules taught in this course was:

"In the chair no auditor has a case. If breath shows on a mirror held to his face he can audit it. Faint afterward if you must..." [40]

This was Hubbard's way of enforcing that illness, or any other excuses we could find, was not acceptable for being late or absent from one's position. It would lead to consequences starting with a visit to the ethics department. Our top priority was to save the planet by making people clear of reactive minds.

Discussing one's emotional state while on duty in the organization could result in severe sanctions and reprimands. A staff member was never supposed to fall below a 2.0 on the Emotional Tone Scale. Any personal issues had to be reported to the ethics officer or the Qualification department and not shared with other staff members or with the public. It was deemed unproductive and Dev-T (developing troubles). I found these rules excessive, but I knew there was no benefit in challenging Hubbard's directives. From then on, my involvement in Scientology became my ultimate priority. Being on staff, I adhered to certain principles that made me a particularly efficient (and stressed) employee. One of Hubbard's mantras—speed of particle flow determines power—was clear: if I wanted to demonstrate my intention to do something, I had to do it as quickly as possible. Operating in that mindset also meant I was 'up-tone,' given that 'Action' was rated 20.0, almost at the top of the Tone Scale. There was something euphoric about staying in that zone, no matter what.

A New Language

Gradually, I became accustomed to the various slogans centered around performance and production, such as *'Production equals morale,' 'Think big,'* or *'Make things go right.'* I realized that, just like in any other business, productivity was key in Scientology. In addition to its tables and charts, this pseudo-science has its own specialized terminology. A few thousand new definitions are found in two Scientology dictionaries: the technical and the administrative dictionaries, spanning around 1000 pages. Terms created by Hubbard describe concepts that exist under different names in other fields, which Hubbard specifically chose not to associate with Scientology, such as psychiatry or psychology. Each day, as I learned new words with meanings unique to Scientology, I delved deeper into this distinct universe. New terms with specific meanings, like Clear or OT, or common vocabulary words, which had particular definitions within Scientology. Innocently, I began using this new language that only Scientologists could understand, further isolating myself from the broader society. From that point on, according to my father, with the "knowledge" I had gained in Scientology's course rooms, I knew more about life at twelve than most 'wogs[41]' out there.

According to him, I now had the tools to succeed and was superior to the average person. Just as children consecrated in The Mission of the Holy Spirit were supposed to be after three or four generations of reincarnation in that movement. On top of all that indoctrination, there were the rants of people who dreamed of one day reaching the state of Clear or OT, fantasizing about a reality unique to Scientology and sharing their beliefs about a parallel world only accessible to OTs. For instance, my father's cousins who came to live with us in St- Michel, whom I helped in the organization's printing room, once told me that a woman I admired in her Navy uniform, who came from the Sea Organization, was high on the "Bridge to Total Freedom" and possessed the powers of an OT, including the ability to read minds. As a teenager, I was impressed.

From that day on, I made sure to be productive in her presence and restrained my adolescent admiration. I started dreaming of becoming a member of the Sea Org myself, living a life of adventure like hers.

The Sea Org

In 1967, Hubbard established a paramilitary organization named the Sea Organization. Many theories have been put forward to explain Hubbard's move or how he presented his projects to Scientologists. However, it is understood that he established this small fleet of two or three boats at the outset to be able to maneuver like a pirate in international waters beyond the reach of any country or government. Once again, he relied on his most fervent admirers— Scientologists who, for the most part, had no experience with navigation but a willingness to follow their guru to the ends of the earth.

'Commodore Hubbard' also created his intelligence agency, the Guardian Office—dedicated to handling legal matters concerning him personally and his Church on land. He appointed his wife, Mary Sue Hubbard, as its head and instructed every member of his 'troops' to study The Art of War, a Chinese military treatise attributed to General Sun Tzu, revived by Mao Zedong with the establishment of the People's Republic of China. Determined to sell as many of his books, courses, and Scientology therapies as possible, he also mandated that members of the Sea Org read Big League Sales Closing Techniques by Les Dane.[42]

This was particularly important for those who went on to establish themselves in various locations, mainly in Europe and English-speaking countries, to create local organizations dedicated to selling Scientology services, especially the advanced levels of Clear and OT. [43]

Living most of the time aboard The Apollo, one of his boats, in the company of his wife Mary Sue and some of his children, Hubbard, surrounded by the Commodore's Messengers—a group of devoted teenage girls—imposed strict disciplinary rules within the Sea Org. He harshly punished those who criticized him, made mistakes, or tried to step out of line, sometimes even throwing them overboard, regardless of their swimming ability. Some would be marked by this treatment for life.

Let's Join the Sea Org

At the Church of Scientology in Montreal, I finally made a few friends my age who, like me, went to the Church of Scientology with their parents.

When my friend Chantal, a girl my age, told me she was leaving Canada to join the Sea Org in Florida with her mother, I decided to join them on this adventure. I wanted to take part with her in the Sea Org's mission to make enough people 'Clear' on the planet, liberating humanity from the negative influence of the reactive mind and the yoke of psychiatry. That same day, I spoke to my parents about my plan, and they agreed to discuss it with the recruiter.

Initially, they were hesitant due to my lack of English skills, but they likely saw this as a preferable alternative to school, which I still refused to attend. Thus, convincing them to let me join the Sea Org was relatively easy. A few days later, I left Montreal with my friend, her mother, my father, and my older sister. We crossed the U.S. border and drove to Burlington to catch a cheap flight to Florida. It would be my first time on a plane, and I was excited to share the experience with my friend.

We landed the next day at Tampa Airport in Florida's warm, humid summer climate. From there, we took a minivan that came to pick us up and took us to the Fort Harrison Hotel, a historic four-star hotel built in 1926 that the organization had purchased a few years earlier. It had become the Flag Land Base.

Establishment of the Sea Organization on Land

In 1975, aging and frail and addicted to drugs, Hubbard ordered his captain to leave the Mediterranean and head toward the Caribbean. He decided it was time to return to dry land and settle on the American continent. Aware that various American government agencies were monitoring them, Hubbard and his followers landed in Florida under the false name 'United Churches of Florida.'

Under this guise, they purchased two commercial buildings in bankruptcy: a fortified building that once housed a bank and the Fort Harrison, an abandoned hotel with eleven floors and approximately two hundred and twenty rooms.

The Sea Org quickly attracted attention and was exposed. However, American opponents of the organization found their efforts in vain: Hubbard and his acolytes were resolute in their determination to establish themselves there, regardless of the obstacles. The Sea Org still inaugurated its Flag Land Base on Fort Harrison Boulevard despite strong criticism from the city's mayor, Gabe Casares, who lost his battle against Scientology. The Guardian Office took measures to silence him and made him pay dearly for his opposition.

CHAPTER 12

ARRIVING AT FLAG LAND BASE

Flag had quickly become the ideal place to deliver the high-priced OT levels of Scientology. It was the 'Mecca' of Scientology, and I was impressed from the moment I arrived. The hotel's majestic character immediately charmed me, making me feel as if I were in a movie surrounded by an aesthetic I had never experienced before. In this place, where everything was designed to make the public feel privileged, I was
enchanted and transported to another world.

In Montreal, I had heard that I might see celebrities since Scientology was known as the religion of the stars. I hoped to meet some of them, as I still dreamed of becoming a performing artist and thought I might find opportunities along the way. However, the only public figure I saw at the Flag Land Base was Leah Remini, who was still relatively unknown at the time. That year, at Flag, just as in the Montreal organization, Scientology promoted L. Ron Hubbard's latest science fiction novel, Battlefield Earth. Posters of Terl, the head of the Psychlos—a sinister and intimidating alien—were displayed in strategic locations. The poster boldly proclaimed under the monster's mouth: 'Psychlos are here.'

Other walls featured posters of Johnny Goodboy, the novel's hero and humanity's last hope. I particularly admired this character, who became a role model for me. While I was still in

Montreal, he ignited my desire to fight the psychs and clear the planet alongside the other members of the 'planetary elite,' the Sea Org. I could already picture myself in a Navy uniform, saluting after returning from an international mission.

During my brief tour of Fort Harrison, I was delighted to discover the outdoor gardens and the in-ground swimming pool, surrounded by comfortable garden furniture. I quickly finished my tour and put on the swimsuit I had packed, eager to dive into the hotel's pool while my father met with the Personal Procurement Officer.

The swim was incredibly refreshing after the long car and plane journey and the endless wait at the airport. I stretched out on one of the deck chairs around the pool. Not having slept all night, I soon numbed under the full sunlight and woke up two hours later with a terrible headache and sunburned as red as a lobster. Feeling miserable, I went to find my father, who was standing in the lobby of Fort Harrison, looking more disappointed and pitiful than I thought. What he told me immediately overshadowed my sunburn. Due to issues related to my father's situation, he could not join the Sea Org. Recruiters would not hire anyone who might be sought by debt collectors or the justice system.

Consequently, I no longer had a legal guardian and could not stay, as Florida law required a legal tutor for someone my age. We had to return with my father. To make matters worse, Dad had not anticipated this and was completely out of money. He didn't even have enough to rent a hotel room, let alone buy plane tickets back to Montreal.

My father decided we would go back to Quebec by hitchhiking, but a Florida State police officer quickly stopped us and insisted we return to Clearwater. Even with my father accompanying me, hitchhiking at twelve years old—especially for a 1500-mile trip—was not allowed. Since my father was willing for me to stay in Florida with my sister, we retraced our steps to Fort Harrison and resolved to persuade one of the recruiters to give me a chance. We knew other twelve-year-old boys were in the Sea Org; I just had to find the right words.

Children in the Sea Org

While the Sea Organization was still navigating, some children were also part of Hubbard's original naval fleet. They were often left on the boats while their parents were busy with their missions on land for the Sea Org or engaged in Scientology auditing and study. These children were put to work and sometimes had to endure Hubbard's temper, facing punishment for disobeying orders or making too much noise. Some were confined to the cabinets used to store the boat's anchor chains, sometimes for entire nights. During this time, Hubbard developed his system of ethics and internal justice, likely to avoid more severe corrective measures like throwing people overboard, which could have led to imprisonment, and to maintain control over his crew. This system allowed him to establish a rigid, totalitarian regime on his boats. [44]

By May 1968, the Sea Org, spread across three boats, had 156 members. As the prerequisites for joining the paramilitary group were relaxed, the number of people on board Sea Org's boats grew rapidly. More couples and families, sometimes with babies, joined the crew. At the peak of this endeavor, which lasted about ten years, the Sea Org's workforce swelled to approximately 450 crew members, stationed on around ten boats sailing between the Californian coast, Denmark, the United Kingdom, and various Mediterranean countries, in addition to those stationed on land. [45]

With a little insistence

Once back at Fort Harrison, I went to the recruiter's office, encouraged by my father, and insisted to a striking red-haired woman that I was worth considering. When she refused, I even started to cry. Perhaps my persistence made her think I was a returning member from a past life, living up to the Sea Org's motto: 'We come back.' Who knows? Either way, she agreed to let me sign the famous billion-year contract, provided I found an adult to act as my legal guardian. My father asked Chantal's mother to take on this role, and thanks to her, I was able to continue my "adventure." I signed the contract, pledging my eternity to the defense of Scientology. In return, they promised several amenities: a decent place to sleep, three meals a day, a uniform as a Sea Org member, training, auditing, and a small stipend of about $20, which I could use to buy a few packs of cigarettes. However, they did not keep their promise, and I found myself in a difficult situation before long!

Discipline

I immediately began the training program required of all recruits, The Estate Project Force (EPF), which subjected us to the level of discipline and submission expected of us in the Sea Org. It involved at least eight to ten hours of manual labor each day, followed by four or five hours of study in a training academy for recruits. The program was running six and a half days a week, leaving us half a day to do our laundry. There was a lot to learn, and we had to prove ourselves worthy of being part of the 'planetary elite.' The program was rigorous, and some candidates chose to drop out before completing it. I recall doing countless push-ups and running around buildings as warm-up or punishment. I wasn't in the best shape and sometimes struggled, but with few options, I persevered, not wanting to return to Montreal. As part of my training, I performed various tasks. I recall cleaning the kitchen of a small restaurant located across Fort Harrison Avenue. Before that day, I had never seen so many cockroaches in my life, and I hope never to again. We also did housekeeping in the rooms of Fort Harrison's paying clients and in some of the rooms occupied by the executives of the many organizations based at Flag.

I remember cleaning the large room reserved for David Miscavige and his wife, Shelly. They held critical positions in Hubbard's inner circle but were rarely present, as they primarily worked in California. Yet, they still had this room reserved for their visits to Florida. Miscavige would eventually take control of Scientology after Hubbard's death a couple of years later. Seeing their superior living conditions compared to mine and those of my three roommates, I began to believe it was possible to rise through the ranks of the Sea Org and hoped for it.

Another memorable task was decorating the large convention hall for the anniversary of the Sea Org's founding. We painted a seascape on large panels to give the impression that the celebration was taking place on the Apollo. When I left Montreal, I had hoped to board the Apollo or another ship, at least occasionally, as I was joining the Sea Org. However, there were no more boats navigating.

Still, I was excited about being part of this grand event. I eagerly anticipated the party, especially when I helped a delivery man unload dozens of boxes of beer and wine into a commercial refrigerator in the kitchen. As I carried the boxes, I wondered if they would let me have a drink, even though I was only twelve. I didn't get the chance to ask, as I wasn't invited to the party yet—I still needed to complete the Sea Org integration program.

A few weeks after our arrival, Chantal and her mother, my 'guardian,' left Flag Land Base for California, where the new international management offices were located. An American who shared my room was assigned to replace Chantal's mother as my legal guardian. I had spoken to him a few times, and he seemed friendly. However, once he was officially appointed as my guardian, he stopped talking to me. He was likely pressured into taking on this role and was now resentful.

Sadly, I quickly realized that I seldom saw my older sister, who had joined the renowned Commodore's Messengers Organization. She lived a few miles from Fort Harrison, where I was stationed, and we were both caught up in work and studies. Initially, I thought we'd embark on this adventure together, but the chance to see her often never materialized.

Despite the loneliness, I fondly remember the summer of 1984. Cindy Lauper, the eternal teenager I adored, was frequently played on Florida's commercial radio stations: "If you're lost, you can look, and you will find me, time after time..." Hearing that song regularly, one I still enjoy today, lifted my spirits. I also dreamed of meeting her on the base, believing Scientology was the religion of stars and celebrities. Fortunately, over time, I made a few friends, even if I only saw them briefly each week. There was the big Swiss man, owner of a chocolate company, who always seemed to have a candy bar or two in his pockets. He would give me a piece every time we met, a small gesture that brought me great joy.

I also have fond memories of a wealthy man from New York who had just joined the Sea Org. He invited me to his wedding, and we spent a wonderful evening on a boat on the canal. That night, I felt more at ease than usual. I recently learned he is still with the Sea Org more than thirty- five years later. Sadly, I doubt we would still be friends today, as I am now considered a Suppressive Person due to my opposition to Hubbard and Scientology.

After a few weeks, I completed the training program and took the oath of allegiance. It was a special day for me, as I would finally be allowed to 'wear the uniform.' I was thrilled to join this group that aimed to redefine the future of our planet and end the oppression of psychiatrists. However, an unfortunate event marred the day. That afternoon, as I walked along Fort Harrison Avenue toward the building where I would be sworn in, a man in a jeep stood up and threw a peach at me. He threw it with the precision of a baseball pitcher, hitting me directly above the knee. I still remember his malicious grin and his arms raised in triumph. Shocked, I quickened my pace to reach my destination and took the oath of allegiance, wondering if such incidents were common for Sea Org members.

Was I targeted specifically, or was I simply in the wrong place at the wrong time? It's plausible that I was the target because of my Sea Org uniform. Scientology faced resistance from Clearwater residents as soon as it arrived in the city in 1975 when Gabe Casares was the mayor. Moreover, in May 1982, the Clearwater City Commission held public hearings following an investigation prompted by numerous citizen complaints.

These hearings led Clearwater to attempt issuing municipal ordinances requiring non-profit organizations to report any allegedly charitable fundraising activities, aiming to counter and reduce fraud. As usual, the Church of Scientology opposed these ordinances and, after prolonged legal battles, succeeded in having them repealed.

When I joined the Sea Org in the 1980s, Scientology and its leaders were also being prosecuted in several countries, including the United States, the United Kingdom, Spain, France, Australia, and Canada.

After my swearing-in, the lovely lady who had recruited me struggled to find a suitable department for me. Being relatively young, I was not easily accepted by the adults, who were preoccupied with their demanding work. However, after exploring several departments, she eventually secured a position for me in the large kitchens of the banquet hall, where the staff took their meals. I worked there with a French-speaking European under the supervision of an American woman who had teenagers of her own in the Sea Org. Unfortunately, she would come to regret having accepted me into her department.

In the kitchen, my main tasks were cracking dozens of boiled eggs each morning and removing loaves of bread from the ovens to slice them with an electric slicer for breakfast. I also prepared dressings, sauces, and gravy, peeled potatoes, cleaned floors and counters, and washed dishes. Occasionally, I had additional duties, like preparing vegetable trays or cutting dozens of heads of lettuce, which I placed in huge bowls and served with French or Italian dressing. The 'Johnny Goodboy' in me didn't find these tasks particularly rewarding. However, I hoped that I could eventually request a transfer to another post and have the opportunity to access a higher position.

One day, I even looked into the eligibility requirements for joining the Commodore's Messenger Org, where many teenagers who had joined the Sea Org ended up, including my older sister. This organization operated directly under Hubbard's orders, and its members were highly respected and considered the elite of the group. I thought it would be the perfect place for me and my ambitions. Maybe Hubbard would even see me as one of his own!

*

In 1971, while the Apollo, the fleet's flagship, was docked in a Moroccan port, the 'Commodore' wrote a letter intended for one of his daughters, Alexis. He had Alexis with his second wife, Sarah Hollister, whom he married while he was still married to his first wife, Margaret Grubb. Hubbard met Sarah Hollister while she was involved in a relationship with Jack Parsons, the leader of the Californian Thelemite lodge of Aleister Crowley, a guy Hubbard watched masturbating for twelve days in a row while he was performing a ritual from one of Crowley's books that was meant to bring back Babalon, the 'Mother of Abominations,' down to earth. [46]

In this letter, the founder of Scientology disowned the young lady, claiming she was someone else's child. That same girl, whom he had allegedly kidnapped about twenty years earlier, was said to resemble him closely, according to several witnesses. Simultaneously, he also disinherited his first son, Ronald Hubbard Jr., who had changed his name to Ronald DeWolf. This disinheritance followed Ronald's involvement in writing and promoting a book that criticized him and Scientology.

In 1974, Quentin, Hubbard's youngest son from his last marriage to Marie Sue, attempted suicide for the first time. His father saw him as his successor and disapproved of his homosexuality. The boy who preferred flying planes and dancing ended his life two years later. He was found unconscious but still alive in a parked car in Las Vegas. The 'Commodore' never publicly acknowledged his son's suicide

Degraded being

I considered applying for the Commodore Messenger Org, but when I learned about their high acceptance standards and the need to rewrite my 'life story,' I abandoned the idea. I also knew I'd have to undergo a rigorous security check with the E-Meter—a device akin to a lie detector used during sessions with auditors. Until then, I had managed to avoid discussing specific episodes of my life. As a Scientologist, I couldn't consider having been abused because Hubbard taught us that we create our own reality through our postulates. So, I had to take responsibility for it.

According to this belief, I was responsible for the events with Sylvio's father since I must have attracted them to myself. For that reason, I tried to accept it and move on. I wanted to forget it. However, I feared I couldn't hide the truth from the ethics officers and the qualifications department if they connected me to the E-Meter. They would discover that I had engaged in sexual activities with another man and label me as gay—something you definitely don't want to be in Scientology.

"Homosexuals are sexual deviants on the same level as pedophiles, and all homosexuals should be sent off to a leper colony."
L. Ron Hubbard, Science of Survival

In short, I knew I didn't qualify, so I stayed working in the kitchens, hoping that someday they would recognize my potential and see that I was more than just someone to crack eggs and wash pots.

Leaving My Body

Because I spoke French, I had the chance to help a student from a French European country finish his auditing course. He would occasionally come to get me in the kitchen so he could bring me to an empty room of Fort Harrison to practice auditing on me. Naturally, I agreed every time, feeling fortunate to receive free auditing and to escape from the confines of the kitchen.

One day, during one of these sessions, I 'returned' to a past life during auditing. In that life, I was a cowboy, complete with a hat and lasso, riding a horse. In this memory, the horse began to buck wildly, reared up, and threw me several feet into the air. Disoriented, I landed on my neck and never got up. I died instantly and began floating above my lifeless body, watching myself lying motionless on the ground. Back in the kitchen, I reflected on the session. I enjoyed reliving these moments when I went outside of my body. Fantasizing about the idea that I was not attached to that soiled body of mine brought me comfort.

CHAPTER 13

ENOUGH IS ENOUGH

One morning in January 1985, a foolish accident in the kitchen turned both my life and that of my superior upside down. That day, I was preparing several boxes of romaine lettuce for lunch. To speed up the process, I used an electric slicer. I held the lettuce in my hand and pushed it toward the rotating blade to slice it. At one point, I lost focus and pushed down too far, cutting off the tip of my right middle finger. Shocked, I wrapped my hand in a rag and went to my superior at the other end of the kitchen, who looked at me with disbelief.

Given the seriousness of my injury, I had to go to a nearby hospital for stitches. On the way, my superior instructed me that no one was to know the true circumstances of my accident. I was to pretend that I didn't speak English, and if someone happened to question me in French, I was to say I was on vacation and had cut my finger with a fishing knife. After that day, everything changed for me at Fort Harrison. According to Hubbard's infallible technology, the accident meant I was a PTS (Potential Trouble Source). Such an event could only result from oppression. Someone in my environment had to be blamed. Hubbard's reference was clear:

"All illness, to a greater or lesser degree, and all foul-ups stem directly and only from a PTS condition." [47]

My American superior, Sarah, whom I dearly loved, was accused of being suppressive and given only two options: register with the Rehabilitation Project Force (RPF) or leave Scientology. She had no choice but to comply; otherwise, she would be expelled from Flag, and her sons would have to choose between their mother and Scientology. This poor woman, who had nothing to do with my accident, would suffer because of my carelessness. My foolishness placed her in a terrible position.

Scientology Goulag

The Rehabilitation Project Force, or RPF, is designed to rehabilitate a Sea Org member who has lost the organization's trust for various reasons: poor performance, failure to adhere to policies, malicious intentions, or criminal activities. The ethics department is responsible for managing the program. Once in the RPF, a person has two main activities: performing demeaning tasks under the orders of an authoritarian and ruthless leader for eight hours a day and undergoing a co-auditing session of about five hours with another RPF member.

Participants in the program are instructed to keep their situation hidden from the public, walking around to avoid drawing attention, but they must run when not in public view. They sleep on mattresses on the floor and can only communicate with other RPF members. Their days are filled with work, leaving them just twenty-minute breaks to eat leftovers after regular Sea Org members have finished their meals. They are required to avoid contact with other Sea Org members and the public at Scientology churches. Several former Sea Org members have compared this reform program, which often extends beyond a year, to the 'gulags'—the infamous forced labor camps of the Soviet Union.

Breaking people

I sometimes saw Sarah picking up trash or scrubbing the floor with a brush. She saw me but never looked at me directly. Each time, it filled me with guilt. I wanted to tell her that I held no grudge and that I never felt oppressed by her. However, she couldn't speak to me unless she had special permission from her superior.

I found this situation disgraceful and unfair. It wasn't Sarah's fault if I wasn't performing well in the kitchen. Why did they want to "break her" like that? In fact, she was one of the few who seemed to care about me. My own poor decisions were tied to the fact that I was almost constantly floating [48]—a state of mind I had experienced more than once over the years. Bored to death in the kitchen, I often dreamed of being elsewhere.

Leah Remini was also assigned to the RPF for allowing a young man to get too close. The same fate befell a young French-Canadian girl who joined the Sea Org around the same time I did. She ended up in the RPF, dressed in old, dirty clothes, forced to clean the public docks and toilets of Fort Harrison, and subsisting on leftover meals because she had the misfortune to fall in love with a young man from the security forces.

It was shocking to see these young girls, who had come to Flag Land Base to participate in the "saving of humanity," end up in such dire straits for trivial matters of the heart. At thirteen, just entering puberty, I couldn't imagine going through adolescence without having the chance to approach one of the beautiful American girls I saw on the site.

When Things Turn Bad

At the start of my adventure with the Sea Org, I envisioned myself actively engaged in missions and fighting the enemy. I had dreamed of participating in operations like the ones I had seen, where people arrived in full uniform at Montreal's Church. But now, here I was, idling in the kitchen with minimal contact with my fellow members, who were all busy with their own tasks. Beginning to miss my family, whom I hadn't seen in nearly eight months, I felt more and more alone. I had received almost no word from my parents or my siblings left in Montreal—not even a Christmas card or a note for my thirteenth birthday, which had passed a few months earlier.

When joining the Sea Org, I had imagined working with the public at Flag and being surrounded by extraordinary individuals like Clears and OTs. Instead, I found myself cracking eggs, cutting bread, mixing salad dressing, and washing floors and pots day after day. I never received the promised twenty dollars a week from my contract and couldn't even afford soap to wash. I was given only two worn shirts and a pair of thick wool pants, uncomfortably hot for Florida's climate, which I had to wear seven days a week. I had expected better. My underwear was in such poor condition that I was embarrassed one of the three strangers I shared a room with might see me in those ragged garments at night. I requested new clothes from the department heads, but my requests went unanswered. So, I had to wash my pants by hand in the bathtub every two or three days before bed, hoping they would dry overnight. One day, I had been furiously kicked out of an office where the public went to receive auditing because I stank from those damned pants that wouldn't dry. That day, I felt a deep sense of shame and knew I had to do something.

Becoming a Traitor

One afternoon in January, I decided to steal forty dollars from the cafeteria cash register. It was the only way I could hold on to a shred of dignity. I didn't see any other option, as talking about my situation to a member of the public—like the Swiss man who sometimes gave me chocolate—would have been considered a serious offense. With that money, I went to a nearby store, bought myself some new clothes, and treated myself to an ice cream cone. That act, to me, marked the end of my career in the Sea Org. I had to betray them just to get a taste of what I felt I deserved.

After some time in the Sea Org, probably following the accident that caused my sympathetic superior's fall, it was decided by the higher-ups that I should integrate into the Cadet Org. This organization, now defunct, was created to take in the children and teenagers of Sea Org members, who were constantly tied up in their duties, working more than a hundred hours a week. The Cadet Org, made up entirely of minors, was supervised by the older members of the group or Sea Org members who had been reassigned to this post as part of their ethics handling.

I was to be moved into a dormitory with other kids, where teenagers would oversee us. They insisted that I study English for about fifteen hours a week in a dismal setting: a room in an old motel, twenty minutes from Fort Harrison. They had thrown together a makeshift classroom there, likely trying to meet the requirements of social services, who were undoubtedly keeping a close watch after the recent investigative commissions. I attended one or two class periods, but the 'Johnny Goodboy' in me decided it was enough. I had come to Florida to fight the enemy—not to be treated like that! In this context, fearing someone would discover I had taken the money in the cafeteria and decided I should be sent to the RPF or thrown out of the Sea Org, I decided it was time for me to leave Flag. At that point, I could not wait to be back home.

I thought about calling one of my older brothers for help, but all the staff phones were monitored. I then attempted to use one of the public phones near the Fort Harrison reception, but Flag's security staff, who were watching me closely, wouldn't let me near them. Each time I tried, they told me the only phones I was allowed to use were in the internal offices. By a stroke of luck, a week or two later, Arthur, a Scientologist I knew from Montreal who was in his early twenties, arrived in Clearwater. I was relieved to see a familiar face and finally had someone to confide in. However, Arthur had committed a crime and was ordered to leave Flag within 24 hours, or else the police would be called. Surprisingly, despite his bad standing, they allowed him to stay on the base and talk to me. This gave me the opportunity to explain my situation. I told him I wanted to run away from there. He then proposed I leave with him that very night. Chatting in the cafeteria, we came up with an escape plan. The security staff were watching me closely, so I had to find a way to leave without them seeing me. A few days earlier, I had scouted a spot where I could jump onto a waste container near a door leading to the kitchen. From there, I could climb over the fence without being seen by the security guards stationed at the entrances. There, I could meet Arthur, who would be waiting for me in a taxi.

Arthur advised me to leave my belongings behind and spend the rest of the day working in the kitchen so as not to raise suspicion. Our plan worked perfectly. I had finally managed to escape from Flag, and for the first time in what felt like forever, I could breathe freely. About thirty minutes later, we were in a motel room near the airport, planning the rest of our trip back to Montreal. However, the relief I felt didn't last long. After getting undressed to go to bed, Arthur tried to have sex with me. I hadn't expected that because he was in a relationship with a female staff member in the Montreal organization when I met him the year before. This time, I firmly refused to let him touch me and was prepared to defend myself to protect my dignity. Anxious, I barely slept that night, ashamed and terrified that Arthur, lying next to me in the same bed, might try again. My mind was in turmoil. I had escaped Flag only to find myself trapped with a predator. I was just thirteen, and Arthur, who turned out to be my only means of escape from Clearwater, knew that. It felt eerily familiar—like Sylvio's father all over again, my 'savior,' that guy who was my only hope of getting back to Montreal, happened to be a pedophile. I could have run away and gone to Clearwater police, but that could have led to me returning to Flag.

Lying there, I struggled to relax after all the stress of the day. Unsettling questions plagued my mind: How had I ended up in the same nightmare again? Did people sense I was easy prey? Was there something about me that attracted this kind of person? And where was Dad again? With my back to Arthur, I silently shed a tear. I was overwhelmed with disappointment as I thought about the year that had passed. I had tried so hard to better my life and improve my situation, putting my heart into the Sea Org's mission. Only to be forced to flee from it. The next morning, Arthur wrote a bad check to an airline to buy us plane tickets to Montreal, with a stopover in Winnipeg. We flew out the same day.

Detour to Western Canada

Fearing interception due to the bad check Arthur wrote, when we landed in Montreal, Arthur decided we would get out of the airport in Winnipeg—still 1,400 miles from Montreal—to find another way home. It was mid-February, and the temperature was around -4°F when we stepped outside. My only clothes were the old blue sports pants with red stripes on the sides, which I had brought from Montreal eight months earlier, and a wool sweater. Arthur, who had winter gear, lent me a pair of socks to wear in my beach sandals. Due to what I wore, I was the laughingstock of a group of young people when we boarded a municipal bus in Winnipeg, but it was worth it—I had left the United States and was back in my country.

After buying a winter coat and boots from a department store downtown, using forged checks as usual with Arthur, we visited Winnipeg's Church of Scientology, hoping for help. But we weren't welcome when we told the Executive director there that I had left Flag the night before. We spent a couple of days in a hotel with no money and nothing to eat. Arthur called a Subway restaurant asking if we could pay an order with a check. They said no—unless we ordered a few dozen.

Soon enough, after requesting to charge a meal from the hotel restaurant to our room, we were confronted by the hotel manager, who insisted that we pay in cash. Since we didn't have any cash on hand, we rushed out of the hotel. As we left, the manager shouted at us that we would share our details with other hotels in the city. From there, it was clear to us that we needed to find different places to stay.

That same day, a guy I think we met at Winnipeg's Scientology church suggested we go to the Gray Nuns of Saint-Boniface, a French-speaking neighborhood in Winnipeg, to ask for shelter. Having no other option, we went there immediately. Once arrived, we told the good sisters we had run away from Scientology in Florida, though we didn't share too many details. They agreed to let me stay while contacting someone in Montreal who could send money for my trip back home and asked Arthur to leave, which allowed me to breathe a little easier.

After that, I reached out to one of my uncles, who had paid for my train ticket to Montreal since Dad was either penniless or simply done with me. I left the convent that same evening, and after a full night's sleep on the train, I arrived in Montreal in the morning. Unfortunately, I learned that while I was planning my escape from Flag, my mother—whom I hadn't spoken to in months—had left Montreal to join the Sea Org with another one of my sisters. I doubt her being in Florida would have changed my decision to leave. However, her presence when I got to Montreal might have made a difference. Unlike my father, she wouldn't have stood by idly after hearing that Arthur had tried to have sex with me.

Only Arthur showed up at Montreal's train station. Somehow, he had managed to reach Montreal before me and had probably learned from my father that I was on that train. That day, he took me to see a magnificent French-Canadian movie by André Melançon, which became a classic: The Dog Who Stopped the War. A story about a group of kids around my age spending their Christmas holiday playing war in a huge snow castle they built.

The memory of watching that movie remains vividly anchored in my mind. It showed me a type of childhood that every French-Canadian child should be able to experience. I fell in love instantly with the film's theme song, "L'amour revient de guerre" (Love Comes Back from War), performed by Nathalie Simard. The song touches me deeply and brings a tear to my eye every time I hear it.

The only thing that marred that experience was Arthur sitting next to me. However, this was one of the last times I had to endure his presence because I didn't stay silent this time. I told everyone around me about the harassment I had endured during the return trip. It was enough to make Arthur flee, fearing arrest by the police.

Yet, despite my outcry, neither Dad nor anyone else took any action against Arthur's despicable behavior. If just one of my parents had taken a stand, it might have helped me understand that what he had done was not only wrong but criminal, something punishable by law. Learning that might have encouraged me to speak up sooner about the abuse I suffered in Saint-Michel at the hands of Sylvio's father.

Persona Non-Grata

At Montreal's Church of Scientology, I was met with hostility and was labeled a deserter from the Sea Org. I was at risk of being officially declared a Suppressive Person if I didn't go to their Canadian headquarters in Toronto to settle matters. So, I hurried to avoid forcing my family members, who were Scientologists, to sever ties with me.

In Toronto, the reception from Sea Org members was even worse than in Montreal. Since I had left without authorization and deserted my post, they assumed I must have had crimes to confess, as per Hubbard's policies. They treated me like a criminal, subjecting me to conditions similar to those in the Rehabilitation Project Force (RPF). I was not allowed to speak to anyone, had minimal food after everyone else had eaten, and was shadowed by a member of the organization while I waited for an auditor to conduct a security investigation and a rigorous interrogation with the pseudo-lie detector called an E-meter.

Fortunately, I was released after a day or two (I still don't remember where I slept) and handed a bill for several thousand dollars for the training courses I had taken at Flag. I was also assigned a rehabilitation program that I would need to complete if I wanted to return to Scientology. Ultimately, my time in Toronto was eye-opening. It made me realize that Sea Org members in Canada endured conditions far worse than what I had seen in Florida, reinforcing my decision to flee the organization and resolve never to return.

Shortly after returning to Montreal, a couple of friends who had joined Scientology at my father's invitation after leaving The Mission of the Holy Spirit also came back from the Sea Org, disillusioned with their experience. In a way, I was relieved to know I wasn't the only one who had 'failed.' The couple had joined together and returned together, both deeply disappointed by their time in the Sea Org. Tragically, the woman lost her unborn child after being denied medical care during her pregnancy, leading to the fetus being flushed down the toilet. They both left Scientology for good and converted to Jehovah's Witnesses.

As for me, I was barred from attending the Church of Scientology until I resolved my situation with the Sea Org. I did not really care since I no longer wished to engage with the Church of Scientology. However, I continued to admire Hubbard's teachings for a long time, as his 'incredible tech' had once helped me detach from my negative emotions and had put me on a pink cloud when I did TRs a year prior. I recall participating in an auditing session with my father as the auditor. During this session, which was mainly a demonstration for one of my cousins, I 'relived' an event from one of my past lives. In it, I found myself in an interplanetary station, lying on an operating table. A scientist in a doctor's uniform and surgical mask stood beside me with surgical tools in his hands, ready to perform an operation on me. He was placing a lamp on my forehead and seemed to be trying to implant thoughts in my mind. I was unsure if he was human or extraterrestrial since he wore a mask.

I loved going into past life like that and firmly believed in it, as Hubbard's literature spoke of implant stations in other galaxies. Once again, I felt privileged to 'travel' in my past universe and validate what I had been taught in Scientology—that we are spiritual beings journeying in physical bodies and that we had lived thousands of lives across the universe. It offered me a different perspective on my life and affirmed that the one I was currently living was just one among many I had experienced and would experience in the future.

CHAPTER 14

TUMBLING

Since joining the Montreal organization's staff eighteen months earlier, I had immersed myself in it almost nonstop, and since arriving at Flag that past summer, I had only been surrounded by Scientologists. It felt like being aboard a warship with my fellow brothers-in-arms, all of us sailing toward the same destination, driven by a shared goal: saving the world through Scientology. Back in Montreal, I felt disoriented and aimless. Banned from the Church of Scientology, I spent a lot of time alone, wandering in Le Plateau. Luckily, with spring's arrival, I managed to lift my spirits. Schools were closed, so I could spend more time with my brothers and cousins, who were now free from their classes. I spent the summer biking and soaking up the warm weather as much as I could. I also started smoking weed more often and drinking low-alcohol drinks. I used to love Durango or Twist Shandy because they were sweet and tasted almost like soda.

By the summer of '85, my mother had already come back from Flag since, like my father, she couldn't join the Sea Org. Back in Montreal, being separated again from my father, she took my two youngest brothers and my three sisters with her, while my two older brothers, aged fifteen and sixteen, resided in a communal house with other older individuals, where drugs and alcohol were abundant. I moved in with my father, with whom I still had a fairly good relationship. He now considered me a Sea Org member 'on a break' and remained proud of me—probably because, up to this point, I was the child who had followed his religious guidelines most closely.

    Still, I spent most of my time at my brother's place since my father was rarely home. In the fall, my cousins and a friend I'd made during the summer returned to school, leaving me alone on my bike rides. I still wasn't going back to the Scientology organization in Montreal, given my status as a Sea Org deserter. Not that I cared anymore—I'd lost interest in Scientology. But I now had to find something else to do with my time by myself, having had the habit of spending my evenings and my weekends in the organization, where a few of my loved ones hung out. Feeling depressed, I started smoking weed and drinking stronger alcohol almost daily, hanging around people who used to hook me up. At that point, I was willing to try just about anything that would freeze my brain for a while. And I was ready to do whatever I had to do to get it!

    One afternoon, my father's girlfriend, a legal secretary who lived with us, asked him if she could take me with her to babysit for her boss since they had to go to the courthouse for a last-minute case. My father had no objections—quite the opposite, really, since I'd have the chance to earn some money. So, we hopped in a taxi, and she and I headed to her boss's house, a criminal lawyer. Once at this man's place, I was greeted by a golden retriever who immediately jumped into my arms as soon as I entered the big apartment. But there were no kids in sight. Surprised, I wondered if they were in the basement or out in the backyard. Silence enveloped the house, leaving me puzzled as I glanced at Dad's girlfriend, who beckoned me to follow her into the apartment. We walked together to the other end of a large flat and entered a room that, judging by its furnishings and the bunk bed adorned with vibrant sheets, appeared to be a children's bedroom. Yet, no children were present. Instead, a man in his fifties greeted me as I stepped inside. He stood naked behind a camera, with only a pair of glasses on his nose. Without hesitation, my father's girlfriend disrobed and settled onto the bottom mattress of the bunk bed, then patted the space beside her, inviting me to join. That day marked my first intimate encounter with a woman, all while her boss filmed us, pausing only to refill his glass with spirits or pulverize hefty chunks of cocaine on a mirrored surface. The criminal lawyer would reach out to me directly the following week, proposing a rendezvous at a downtown hotel with a different escort—for a modest sum.

During this chapter of my life, my misery intensified to suffocating levels. To numb my emotions, I consumed about any narcotic or pill within reach, desperately seeking escape. One endless afternoon, I swallowed a dozen Dilantin tablets—an epilepsy medication. I'd spotted the bottle, belonging to my father's girlfriend, a notorious addict, atop the fridge. Desperate to escape my feelings, I thought these pills might do the trick. That woman was always stoned, and I figured that these were the miraculous pills. I began by swallowing one." ... then two... three... feeling nothing. Not 'taking off,' I kept popping them until something happened, until I lost consciousness. I came back to life in an ice-filled bathtub, jolted by a cop's screams and slaps. Naturally, he notified Youth Protection. Weeks later, a social worker investigated, discovering my two-year school absence and my parents' helplessness. As autumn classes began, I found myself before a Youth Chamber judge, who sentenced me to a year in Juvenile Detention.

The Center

Early in my stay at the institution, I often found myself crying at night. Confined to my cramped room, memories of Florida and Flag frequently surfaced, sometimes sparking regret for my escape. At least in the Sea Org, despite experiencing solitude, it granted me relative freedom. Now, I was trapped, surrounded by psychoeducators and psychologists—Johnny Goodboy's sworn enemies. Eventually, I acclimated to this new reality. Abstaining from drugs and alcohol, my health rebounded, and I resumed schooling. Gradually, I recognized the psych staff's genuine desire to help, allowing myself to open up slightly. Still, I viewed them as misguided pawns of a larger suppressive system bent on global control.

Once permitted, my mother visited regularly, eventually bringing me home for weekends. We'd stroll to the subway, conversing more than ever before. One day, waiting on the platform, we had an unforgettable exchange. As the lead carriage rumbled in, Mom raised her voice: *"You know I love you more than anything, you and your siblings!"*

I smiled, grasping her hand as the train neared. She locked eyes with me, adding, *"If not for my love for you, I'd have thrown myself in front of one of these trains long ago."* Her words left me flustered and speechless. A moment, steeped in profound sadness, that still unsettles me today.

Helpless, I remained silent, grasping the depth of Mom's despair. At her house, an urge to flee overwhelmed me as if her presence was unbearable. After dropping my bag, I'd vanish until late at night, returning utterly stoned. This pattern repeated every visit, and after a few weekends, my mother refused to host me again.

For months, I spent weekends at the center, lacking alternatives. Fortunately, Carmen and Serge, one of my father's friends and his partner, with whom I got on well, eventually visited. They offered occasional stays until they had a child. Afterward, since she had to take care of her baby, I was back to center-bound weekends. In October 1985, my sentence was due to end, but having failed to show my 'ability to function in society,' relapsing into drug use and clashing with fellow residents, the Youth Chamber judge was petitioned to extend my stay another year.

The following summer, my mother agreed to take me back, anticipating my official 'release' that fall. However, she departed for another U.S. stint, this time at a Scientology outfit in California. Geneviève re-entered our lives, agreeing to a two-week watch. Mom's absence stretched to a month and a half. That poor Geneviève—I'll never forget her—who expressed that abandoning their children for supposed 'religious' reasons was unacceptable, got a taste of Scientology's 'medicine.' Instantly branded a suppressive person and enemy of Scientology, Mom banished her from our lives despite her month-and-a-half vigil over us, depleting her savings in the process!

My summer at my mother's place ultimately flopped. I was no angel: daily drug use and a knack for trouble defined me. Fearing my influence on my younger siblings, Mom refused custody upon my release. Barred from my father's, and with Serge and Carmen focused on their newborn, the center's psycho-educators proposed a foster family. I flatly refused—I already had a family, unwelcoming as it was. So, I remained at the center until my eighteenth birthday.

Fortunately, the educators at the center were lenient with me: as I grew older, I enjoyed increasing freedom. They allowed me to go out on weekends without probing about where I'd be spending the night. Usually, I crashed at my brother's place. We often drank and smoked weed while listening to Black Sabbath or Iron Maiden. We weren't exactly saints. I stole to get what I needed, which was about more than just food this time. I swiped many bicycles until my own, which I cherished, was stolen. After that, I quit stealing, afraid that some kind of karma might hit me even harder next time.

Cursed

Sometimes, I would visit my mother, since, after all, I was still her son. One day, she asked me to let my two older brothers know that we needed to go to a restaurant around the corner from her place to meet one of her brothers. We hadn't seen him since he returned to The Mission several years earlier. That same uncle who had briefly left The Mission with us about ten years ago, with whom we celebrated our first Christmas, had previously arranged with my mother to meet us there.

Happy to hear that this once-adored uncle wanted to see us again, we cheerfully accepted the invitation and left my brother's place together to walk the few blocks that separated us from the restaurant. However, on the way to the meeting, we wondered about the reason for his visit: why had he reached out after almost ten years without even a phone call? Had he left the damned cult? We were anxious to find out. Personally, I was expecting to face another rejection like the one I experienced at my aunt's place as a kid, but I did not talk about it with my brothers, as if I didn't want to provoke destiny.

When we arrived at the restaurant, it quickly became clear from my uncle's severe demeanor that this meeting wasn't just a courtesy call. He had a specific agenda: to persuade us to join him at an assembly taking place in a nearby corner that same evening. Seeing that none of us had any intention of going with him, he left, expressing his disappointment and predicting a bleak future for us. What a shame! For years, that uncle had attended assemblies two blocks from Mom's house but never bothered to visit or even say hello to his sister or us.

I was deeply disappointed and shaken. I'd already experienced this kind of treatment from my father's sisters nearly ten years earlier. Now, I was being condemned again, this time by a member of my mother's family. It seemed like these relatives were determined to strip us of our freedom by imposing the seclusion of that movement on us. Again, I was strongly disappointed by my mother. Why did she put us in such a shameful situation? She must have known her brother would try to convince us to follow him: had she given up on us? Did she think it would be better for us to return to that cult she had fought so hard to rescue us from, thinking we would never find our place in the outside world?

My years at the center weren't easy. There, I was constantly surrounded by psychoeducators, whom I viewed a bit like the monsters in Battlefield Earth—people I had to be wary of. Although I no longer considered myself a Scientologist, I frequently clashed with them, convinced they were on the wrong side. Believing myself different and superior because of my religious upbringing and my 'fantastic knowledge of the human mind,' I isolated myself with my judgmental attitude, making it hard to form friendships. Filled with anger and frustration at my situation, I often confronted other young people, who finally ended up beating me up.

Becoming an Adult

Looking back on this period of my life, I admit that those four years at the center were the best thing that could have happened to me at the time. I'm grateful to the Quebec system, which, despite its shortcomings, took good care of me during those turbulent years. Thanks to my placement, I found relatively welcoming and appropriate supervision for a lost teenage boy like I was. The educators, dedicated and strong enough to challenge me, had the authority to help me steer onto a 'healthier' path. At the center, I participated in a lot of team sports, something I had never done at home. I often found myself sitting on the bench and rarely scored points, but it made me socialize and helped me feel less isolated. With my artistic temperament, I occasionally managed to express and externalize my emotions through various forms of arts activities organized by the educators.

Thanks to my placement, I also learned a trade that paid well and received help finding a job. I even started working full-time before I left the center at eighteen. I was working as a metal tool worker and already earning a good living. The job didn't suit my personality, but it paid well enough for me to afford an apartment and buy what I needed. For a certain time, I would miss the tight supervision I was used to at the center, but overall, the transition went smoothly. While working in that monotonous environment, which I would eventually come to despise, my childhood dreams resurfaced. I rediscovered the same sense of fulfillment I had found at the center through various art forms. At the center, I had sung occasionally for fun with a guy who played guitar, but now, with a decent salary, I could invest in proper singing lessons and theater classes—my newly rediscovered passion. I also began singing in a Catholic church after an elderly lady recommended me to the parish organist. I thought, "Why not?"

Even though I wasn't baptized in that faith, I saw it as a great opportunity to find an audience and work on my stage fright. I was hired on the spot and left the church with music to prepare for the following Sunday's service. Before long, I led masses and performed on Easter and Christmas. Despite knowing almost nothing about Christianity and not being a believer, I loved singing for people who appreciated it. Unlike my father, who harshly criticized the Catholic Church, I approached this new experience with an open mind. I quickly became the target of derogatory remarks from those in my circle who had grown up in The Mission or were Scientologists. Nevertheless, I continued singing in church almost every Sunday. I was surprised by how some ex-members of The Mission harbored a deep hatred for the Catholic Church, even though they had never interacted with it and had left The Mission years ago. They had been 'educated' to feel this way. Some Scientologists I knew that encountered on the streets near their organization didn't hate the Catholic Church as intensely but still dismissed it as a ridiculous deception.

Although I wasn't Catholic myself, I disliked their attitude, especially since Scientology claimed that everyone, regardless of their beliefs or religion, was welcome in its churches. Years later, I discovered that Hubbard presented himself as the Antichrist in the confidential OT 8 materials. He had taken it upon himself to destroy Christianity, which he denounced as a grand deception. He stated in these materials that:

> "The historical Jesus was not nearly the sainted figure he had been made out to be. In addition to being a lover of young boys and men, he was given to uncontrollable bursts of temper and hatred that belied the general message of love." [49]

Hoping for a better future

In 1992, feeling miserable at the factory where I worked, I resigned from my position. The psychologist at the Center had suggested 'metal tool working' for me, one of the very few options available at the Juvenile Center, because she considered it was the trade that would better suit me. However, even though the pay was good, I didn't like it since I was not a shop-type guy.

At just twenty years old, I was already fed up with working in that kind of environment. I still had my whole future ahead of me and wasn't about to waste it there. Since I left the job voluntarily, I wasn't eligible for unemployment insurance, so I had to apply for social assistance. To get my life back on track, I enrolled in adult school with the help of social services, aiming to obtain my high school diploma. However, things spiraled, and I found myself facing poverty again. I lived in rooming houses in dismal neighborhoods, and my living conditions deteriorated daily. Eventually, I ended up without a permanent address, living with a woman named Denise, who was at least twice my age, whom I met at a friend's place, where she came to buy marijuana. I mentioned my singing at the church near her home, and she came to see me at the following Sunday service. She then invited me to lunch at her place. We hit it off, and I ended up staying there all day and night… We had a blast together, often partying, using marijuana and alcohol daily, and doing cocaine on weekends, usually at Denise's expense. We spent a week in Acapulco and crossed the border to the United States a few times, driving south to Atlantic City and other spots near Quebec's border. Without a job, I spent most of my time watching TV, strumming the guitar in Denise's living room, and singing at the local Catholic Church on Sundays. Life was pretty good for a while… until I wanted to leave.

CHAPTER 15

ALONE IN THE CROWD

In June 1993, the Montreal Canadiens won their 24th Stanley Cup. A couple of days after that victory, on June 11th, a parade was scheduled to pass down Sherbrooke Street, allowing fans to greet their 'Glorious' players. That day, as I leaned on the ramp watching the crowd gather in the distance, I found myself reflecting on my life. A few days earlier, I had met a girl my age, and it made me realize I no longer wanted to be with Denise. Yet, I felt unable to leave her. Dysfunctional, I clung to Denise like a child clinging to his mother on the first day of school. I was paralyzed by a fear of life and had nowhere else to go. To distract myself, I decided to join the crowd waiting for the parade, not knowing I'd never forget the feeling I would experience that day. I walked briskly and arrived before the parade, which was still a few blocks away.

Approximately 600,000 people filled the streets, cheering with joy. When the Stanley Cup finally appeared, held aloft by our goalie, Patrick Roy, the crowd around me erupted in wild cheers. Not being a big hockey fan, I looked at them without understanding what made them go mad like that. Unexpectedly, as I looked around at the jubilant faces, I felt an immense void opening up in my chest. Standing there in the massive crowd, I felt a suffocating sense of death boiling inside me. I felt utterly alone and insignificant amidst the sea of people, so I left immediately to return to Denise's place. Once at her place, I went back to the balcony from which I had watched the crowd gather before the parade. The weather was amazing on that glorious day. However, things weren't so great for me. This time, I wasn't watching the crowd cheer. Instead, I was looking down at the sidewalk, gauging the height and imagining what state I would end up in if I jumped from the fifth-floor railing.

Looking down, I saw the image of my broken body lying in a pool of blood. I realized that this 'vehicle' I had borrowed for twenty-one years would be beyond repair. My thoughts then drifted to friends I had known who had chosen to end their lives in the past years— Dany, Francis, Jocelyn—all around my age. I understood that dying was an option since they had chosen it. I wondered if they were now happier, in limbo, or suffering in hell for eternity. Had they already reincarnated, carrying with them the suffering they sought to escape? I also thought of my siblings: how would they cope with my decision if I were to make it? Would they one day follow in their older brother's footsteps? If I chose to end my life, it would also imply to them that it was a viable option. Projecting myself in the future made me realize that my life could signify something to other people in my life, even though it didn't for me.

That afternoon, I clung to life by recalling moments of happiness I had experienced in my childhood. I reminded myself that I had dreams and some talents and that if I persevered, I might achieve something with them. I found enough hope to step away from the concrete railing, trying to banish the image of my broken body from my mind. I shed a few tears, feeling a deep inner pain, before falling to my knees and sending a prayer into the universe, asking for help. I had never done that in my life, but I had seen many people in that position at the church where I sang, so I told myself I had nothing to lose by trying. I didn't believe in it, but I still closed my eyes and mumbled a few words, simply asking to be happy in life and to fulfill my ambitions. After a few moments on my knees, I regained my senses. As I opened my eyes and saw my reflection in the patio door, I quickly stood up, feeling absurd and out of character. I hadn't been raised to act this way. I went into the apartment to grab a beer and roll a minuscule joint, just like Dad used to do. I had almost stopped smoking weed recently because it was making me paranoid. My eyes turned so red that I wouldn't even dare walk in the corridor of Denise's building without sunglasses on.

Under Influence

In the evening, as I chatted with Denise, I avoided mentioning the balcony incident. Instead, I discussed my moods, expressing my unhappiness and desire to make a change in my life. I told her I needed to leave and find someone my own age, thinking she would not really mind. However, without missing a beat, Denise looked at me and said, *"You're not ready to go yet."*

I was stunned by her words and didn't know how to respond. I felt a twinge of offense but kept silent. Instead, I took another sip of beer and changed the subject, trying to process what she had said. It was the first time she had spoken to me that way, as if she had authority over my life and could decide what I should do with it. We let it go, continued with the evening as if nothing had happened, and went to bed early since Denise had to work the following day. However, that night, as I lay beside her in her king-size bed, I woke up crying from a terrible nightmare. In the dream, I was in bed next to Denise, who was clawing at my leg to pull me toward her. The pain from the burning tips penetrating my flesh jolted me awake. I turned to her and saw that her skin was gray and dry, and she was staring at me with bright, demonic red eyes. I felt like I had seen the 'devil himself.' Terrified, I immediately got up and took refuge in the living room, where I stayed for a while. I wasn't a true believer, but feeling lost and not knowing what else to do, I reached for the large Bible Denise kept on the coffee table and held it close to my chest for comfort and protection. I couldn't shake the memories of the terrible day I had and the things Denise had said to me. It was becoming clear to me that she had a strong psychological hold on me. I had become so dependent on her in every aspect of my life, and it made me feel pitiful. I knew that I had to make significant changes, even though I felt completely powerless.

After an hour or so, I tried to sleep on the sofa, unwilling to return to bed with Denise. However, after a while, I went back to the bedroom and found that she had regained her normal appearance. Realizing that it was only a nightmare, I climbed back into bed. Unable to sleep, I drifted off just before dawn, only to wake up a couple of hours later. Fortunately, Denise had already left for work by the time I woke up around ten, sparing me the need to discuss my decision with her. Still upset, I got out of bed with only one thought in mind: to leave and never return. It would take courage to leave everything behind me, but there was no other way out of my situation. Without knowing where I would go, I dressed and left the apartment with the firm resolve not to set foot there again. As I stepped out of the elevator and onto the ground floor, I felt anxious and unsure of where I was headed. However, as soon as I reached the sidewalk, I saw my friend Daniel, whom I hadn't seen in ages, standing on the other side of the street. It was as if he was waiting for me to get out of Denise's building. He saw mw called out, "*Laflèche! Is that you?*" I stood there, speechless, staring at him from a distance, amazed to see him there. My friend was definitely not an angel; however, that day, it was as if he had come from heaven just to intercept me! He waved at me as I crossed the street, so I happily approached him and asked what he was doing there. It had been a couple of years since I had last seen him. He told me that he was heading to a support group meeting for people with addictions and invited me to join him. With nowhere else to go and no money in my pockets, I didn't hesitate and accepted his invitation to walk with him to the support group. On our way, Daniel proudly told me he had stopped using drugs for more than a year. I didn't say a word, as I couldn't understand why he had made such a decision.

A new way of life

There were people smoking cigarettes outside the meeting. They all seemed nice and welcomed me with open arms as if I was already a member of their group. I immediately felt at ease, so I decided to walk in and sit down to listen to the people talking. Many of the stories I heard sounded similar to mine. They spoke about a new way of life they had discovered, one of living clean and sober. It resonated with me and made me realize that, like them, I no longer found any enjoyment in using drugs. I then decided to quit using and drinking too, excited by the new horizon that was promised to me. That night, I didn't return to Denise's place; instead, I slept on a public bench in Lafontaine Park, across from her apartment. When Daniel learned about my situation, he offered me a spot on his sofa, giving me the time I needed to gather my thoughts and find a new place to live.

At first, it took me a while to wean off and find restorative sleep. Fortunately, I didn't have to go through a terrible withdrawal like those shooting heroin do. At night, I often thought about my maternal grandmother. I could almost feel her presence, watching over me with a tender gaze, finally proud of me. I loved her deeply and hadn't seen her as often as I wished while she was alive, partly because she had returned to The Mission of the Holy Spirit. Despite her involvement in the cult, Grandma Simone was one of the few who continued to make an effort to visit us. Sadly, towards the end of her life, she was kept away from us by one of my uncles, who didn't want us on his property.

After a couple of weeks of being clean, I returned to Denise's place with a friend I had met in my support group. He had a car, so he helped me retrieve a cardboard box and a bag containing all my belongings, which I had left at her place. It meant a lot to me because, at that point in my life, breaking free from Denise's hold was more important for me than whether or not I would remain abstinent for long. Around the time I left her and stopped using drugs and alcohol, I began writing song lyrics. The feelings I had repressed with substances started to surface. I picked up my guitar and set these words to music. Without realizing it, I was tapping into my inner world; what emerged was far from joyful.

The Neighborhood Kid

You, the neighborhood child, next-door neighbor, I saw you cry.
You who left school, overcome by the mad desire to follow an idol.
Listen to your heart, and talk to me about it,

Don't be ashame, come and find me, because somewhere in you is hidden a part of my past.

The Unbalanced

I'm unbalanced, I often have an aftertaste of letting go of everything, because my head is racing like crazy.

I had unknowingly embarked on a healing journey that would take years to reach fruition. The upheavals I'd experienced in the heart of the Montreal Canadiens supporters' crowd had opened a breach from which I was drawing—more or less unconsciously—my song lyrics.

Chronic depression

By the winter of 1995, I had been free of alcohol and drugs for eighteen months. Thanks to my new way of living, I was finally transitioning into adulthood and becoming more independent. My chance meeting with Daniel, who seemed to be standing on the sidewalk like an angel sent to guide me, had been providential. I saw it as a message from the universe: I had to stop using drugs. So, I took the hand extended to me in those meetings. All I had to do was to go with the flow, and soon enough, I found myself on solid ground.

Still, while my new lifestyle and friends had helped me get back on track, it wasn't enough to fill the emptiness that had lingered since June 1993. I hadn't yet shaken the darkness that seemed to float in my chest permanently. Simply stopping my consumption wasn't enough to fix things: I would have needed therapy. One morning, in the depths of Quebec's winter, with its short, dark days, my mind went black again. Indoctrinated by childhood beliefs, I outright rejected the idea of seeking professional help. Even though I had seen firsthand during my teenage years that the psycho-educators and psychologists I dealt with at the Juvenile Center had never wished me harm, a deep-seated distrust toward anyone with a 'psych' title persisted.

Once in a while, I saw my father, and we'd have lunch or coffee together. When I mentioned my state of mind, he suggested

I try Scientology's therapy. At first, I hesitated to return, knowing I had an enormous ethics program to complete before I could be readmitted. However, he explained that the previous year, Scientology's international management had declared a general amnesty. All former Scientologists who had been declared 'suppressive persons' or who were assigned a major ethics program like the RPF could quickly be rehabilitated and return to Scientology services, such as processing sessions or any type of courses if they wished. Under these new conditions, maybe I could give Scientology a chance to prove itself—to show me that it could actually do what it prided itself on—restore my ambition and give me hope for a better life!

Upon entering the Montreal Scientology organization with my father, who was thrilled to see me returning, something 'miraculous' happened just as I passed the door: I immediately felt better, stepping back into the Scientology 'universe.' The Creed displayed in the hall, declaring that the spirit controls everything, gave me hope and suggested my body was secondary. Then, entering an office where I stumbled on the Tone Scale, with its little thetans seemingly inviting me to join them at the top, I was almost brought back automatically into that zone of emotions I'd floated in while practicing TRs ten years before.

It was all there—the upbeat staff, much more welcoming than they had been when I left the Sea Org at thirteen. This time, I wasn't treated like a deserter since most of the new staff had no idea who I was. In the Qualification department, they only asked me to write down any destructive actions I might have committed regarding Scientology during my absence. I also had to sign a few papers, agreeing not to revisit any old grievances I'd had with the church—something like that. All of this would be recorded in my ethics file, and after that, I could re-enter the church and sign up for a course or audit processes.

I knew that in my first encounters with staff members, someone would try to recruit me for the staff of Montreal's org, so I made sure to tell them I had been in the Sea Org; because of that, I couldn't be recruited by a lower-level organization. Then, to make sure the Sea Org's recruiter didn't try to bring me back, I told them that during my years of hardship, I had taken LSD. Because of that, I could never return to the Sea Org, as per Hubbard's policy, anyone who has taken that drug is barred from being a member of the organization. (Those were the rules back then. However, it may have changed by now, given the difficulty they face in recruiting new members.)

From then on, the staff gave me much more consideration—but I would have to pay for it. That was fine with me! Since I'd stopped using drugs eighteen months earlier. I quickly returned to work as a metal tool worker, built up some savings, and established a solid credit record.

A Church?

The course and auditing registrar, a woman in her forties, didn't know me—she hadn't been a Scientologist when I attended the church as a teenager. But she did know I was the son of a well-known Scientologist. She began the interview as she would with any newcomer. Familiar with much of the jargon she was using, I interrupted her and said, "I want to learn more about God." I knew Scientology didn't really concern itself with God, but I wanted to push the conversation further. Ever since, I found myself on my knees on that balcony, praying to I didn't even know who or what, to see my life change drastically within 24 hours I'd been questioning everything. I wasn't sure of anything anymore. My fragile beliefs about spirituality— mostly shaped by Scientology, which denies the idea of a God—were starting to crumble.

The registrar clearly hadn't expected me to bring up God, which surprised me, considering we were in what was supposed to be a church. She told me that by crossing the Bridge to Total Freedom—the spiritual path outlined by Hubbard, leading to the states of Clear and OT—I'd eventually learn more about the concept of God and come to my own conclusions on the subject. More or less convinced, I let her continue her 'sales pitch.' She pointed out a large poster, which I already knew, pinned to the wall: The Grade Chart. This table, which I had barely glanced at ten years ago, mapped out the entire journey to Clear and OT. She explained that there were two ways to ascend that Bridge. The first option involved purchasing auditing processes, which would be delivered by a professional auditor within the organization—an option that initially appealed to me. However, I realized I didn't have the means since, at that time, it required around $100,000 just to reach the state of Clear, with hundreds of thousands more needed to attain the highest OT levels.

She then offered me a second, much cheaper option: becoming an auditor myself and progressing through each stage of the Bridge by co-auditing with another auditor. I opted for this route and signed up for a pack of three courses starting the following week. I paid about $3,500, including tax, which seemed like a reasonable alternative to the first option.

Since there were other people born in The Mission of the Holy Spirit, in Scientology, bearing the same name as mine, I seized the opportunity to shed a name I disliked and became Michael Laflèche Francoeur. Not Michel Laflèche, but Michael Laflèche, because it sounded more like an English-speaking actor—think Tom Cruise or John Travolta. With Scientology being the religion of the stars, I figured I'd play along! Little Laflèche would now have to 'go hide, so I also stashed my song lyrics in the closet as I began to view them as too 'low tone.' I'd no intention of revisiting that emotional zone far below 2.0 on the Scientology Tone Scale —a major mistake I'd regret many years later, because the little voice inside me, who had found a breach and inspired those lyrics, would not stay silent for long.

The next day, after settling the bill with the treasury, I entered the grand academy. From now on, I'd be studying in the room where auditors trained, a prospect that thrilled me since I'd never been allowed in there as a kid. This was where we delved into Hubbard's technology, which was meant to lead to the state of Clear and OT and elevate people to new levels of consciousness and existence.

CHAPTER 16

THE GREAT ACADEMY

Sitting in the big academy filled me with pride. However, my excitement quickly faded as I started reading the first pages of the major course on the subject of study: "The Student Hat." It reminded me of a situation from ten years ago when I ended up in the ethics office for disagreeing with something I had read in one of the first bulletins in the course, a document titled "Student's Guide to Acceptable Behavior." It outlined the various rules we were expected to follow while studying at the academy. From the start, I encountered some I wasn't ready to commit to:

"You must get permission from the Office of L. Ron Hubbard to leave the course before you are allowed to leave. You won't be released if there is any doubt that you are technically inadequate or that your case is considered poor. Give an advanced warning as to when you are leaving."

Reading these lines, I wondered if I had ended up in some mental institution where one needs a doctor's approval to leave. I wasn't ready to surrender my right to withdraw from the course if I disagreed with its content.

Additionally, I learned that my freedom would be further restricted until I completed the course, which would last at least a few weeks. Completing the courses in the package I had just purchased would take several months:

"Do not consume or have administered to yourself or any other student any drug, antibiotics, aspirin, barbiturates, opiates, sedatives, hypnotics, or medical stimulants for the duration of the course without the approval of the Director of Training."

If I followed the rules, I would be barred from attending another church or participating in any other therapy without the approval of an authorized person in the organization, including my meetings.

"Do not engage in any rite, ceremony, practice, exercise, meditation, diet, food therapy or any similar occult, mystical, religious, naturopathic, homeopathic, chiropractic treatment or any other healing or mental therapy while on course without the express permission of the Director of Tech or the ethics officer."

I was taken aback when I read that I couldn't attend other religious services since Scientology claimed its followers could practice another religion at the same time. Given that I was still singing in Catholic churches and taking part in the rituals as a performer on the altar, I wondered if this would be a problem. Would I need to seek permission for that? Then, I discovered that I I had to agree to a sort of 'law of silence.':

"Do not discuss your case, your auditor, your supervisors, your classmates, L. Ron Hubbard, HCO WW personnel or HCO WW with anyone. Save your unkind or critical thoughts for your processing sessions or take up complaints with any supervisor."

From what I read there. I wasn't allowed to discuss my concerns or doubts about their rules or the courses, with anyone except representatives designated by the Church of Scientology! Sitting in my chair, I reflected on my time in the introductory course room. How they had imposed the 'technology of study' on me, eventually sending me to the ethics department because I said I did not agree with what Hubbard had written. Then, they encouraged me to change my perspective and join the ranks. They had asked me to surrender my critical thinking and personal freedoms.

Totalitarianism

In another document, titled "Keeping Scientology Working," I discovered that Hubbard's writings were considered unalterable. It was strictly forbidden to modify or add to this 'religious philosophy,' even if it meant improving it.

"Our technology was not discovered by one group. (...) We will not speculate here on why this was so or how I came to rise above the bank. We are dealing only in facts and the above is a fact: the group left to its own devices would not have evolved Scientology, but with wild dramatization of the bank called "new ideas" would have wiped it out. The common denominator of a group is the reactive bank."

Hubbard claimed he had taken on the responsibility of implementing this technology flawlessly, against all odds and tides. And he had done it:

"An individual must rise above an avid craving for agreement from a humanoid group to get anything decent done."

We couldn't contribute to improving it, not even try to, by bringing something interesting to Scientology's attention because Hubbard was dead, and it was forbidden to change anything in his material. He had to be the one who overcame the infamous reactive mind, also known as the bank—this 'design flaw' of the human mind supposedly responsible for all the world's problems. According to his teachings, only Hubbard had been able to tame it. Without him, 'humanoids' were left to their own devices and bound to fail. His rhetoric was totalitarian and completely clashed with my values. I believed in fellowship and in the idea that everyone could contribute to making the world a better place.

"I don't see how popular measures, self-sacrifice, and democracy have done anything for man except to sink him further into the mud."

Hubbard sought to establish a system where he was the sole master on board. But that wasn't going to fly with me. Keeping my back straight and a smile on my face, I waited for the study period to end. Then, I'd head to the registrar and tell her I'd changed my mind—I wanted a refund. Once in her office, the registrar informed me I'd have to follow certain procedures, which included, among other things, meeting the ethics officer. That would've dragged me into a long series of bureaucratic hoops. So, I told her flat out that I didn't intend to get bogged down in piles of paperwork. All I wanted was my money back and to leave quietly. I reminded her that Quebec laws protected consumers in situations like this. And I added, without hesitation, that I wouldn't shy away from getting a lawyer involved if necessary to get my $3,500 back.

Without batting an eye, she shot back that threatening the Church of Scientology with legal action was considered a major crime. I could be declared a suppressive person on the spot. That would seriously affect my loved ones who wanted to stay in Scientology since they'd be PTS if they kept in contact with me. If they wanted to continue their courses or processing, they'd have no choice but to cut ties with me. Feeling trapped, I slammed the door on my way out, telling her they would be hearing from me. Distraught, I went home, lighter in my wallet, knowing I'd disappointed my father. I was also disappointed in myself for having to leave the Church of Scientology—a world I'd barely entered but one that had made me feel so good.

A few weeks later, after receiving countless calls from the Montreal organization—and under my father's relentless pressure—I found myself, yet again, pitifully sitting in the ethics officer's office. Frustration gnawed at me. I couldn't get my refund without clashing with the Church of Scientology, which meant risking the loss of ties with my Scientologist relatives. I was also stuck in a deep mental dilemma: how could I feel my spirits lift the moment I stepped into Scientology's universe, even though I hadn't done anything new in Scientology for years?

Confused and unsure which way to turn, I chose to ignore my growing realization about Hubbard's true nature. After all, I felt good in that environment, where everyone was always so 'up-tone.' In that place where that persistent void inside me, the one that had been gnawing at me lately seemed to vanish the moment I entered. Why keep insisting on staying true to myself if the price was this much pain? Why confront that gaping hole inside me when I could just disconnect from it? Feeling pitiful, I asked to be allowed to complete the courses I had already paid for, promising to follow the rules. They agreed, but because I had dared to threaten legal action, I was required to write an affidavit requesting permission to resume the classes I'd wanted to leave. Then they demanded I purchase twenty-five hours of professional auditing to undergo a rigorous security check, referred to as a 'Confessional.'

Hubbard-Style Confession

The process I was about to undergo was called the 'Johannesburg Confessional.' Developed by Hubbard during his time in South Africa, it's a key part of Level 2 on the grade chart. It forms an essential step on the famous Bridge to Total Freedom, supposedly leading to the 'state of Superman.' This process is supposedly designed to help the Scientologist 'get their ethics in' by forcing them to confess any destructive acts they may have committed in the past, especially those involving Scientology. However, it has nothing to do with a Catholic confession since the auditor notes down everything the person says and sends it to the Ethics department and to the case supervisor.

The auditor asks questions about actions deemed harmful by or to the organization and actions the Scientologist might have committed or could still be committing.

It begins with a list of questions, starting with:

> *Are you here to investigate Scientology?*
> *Do you have a criminal record?*
> *Did you give me your real name?*

The auditor writes all the answers in a report that is sent to different individuals in the organization, who then sometimes insist that the Scientologist address certain situations or behaviors before continuing their ascent on the Bridge. Naturally, all reports generated during the Confessional are stored in different files, notably in the ethics file of the person being interviewed.

I began my 'Confessional' with a professional female auditor in the spring of 1995. I was excited to receive what I considered auditing, as it was part of the grade chart. Still, the thought of confessing to a woman made me a bit uneasy. From the start, I had high expectations for my sessions, having often seen people leave those rooms beaming from ear to ear with smiles. I anticipated something similar, and I was fully committed to the process, determined to spill everything.

The confessional took place in a small room, where all auditing is conducted using an E-meter, a device that supposedly reads people's emotions related to what is going on in their minds.

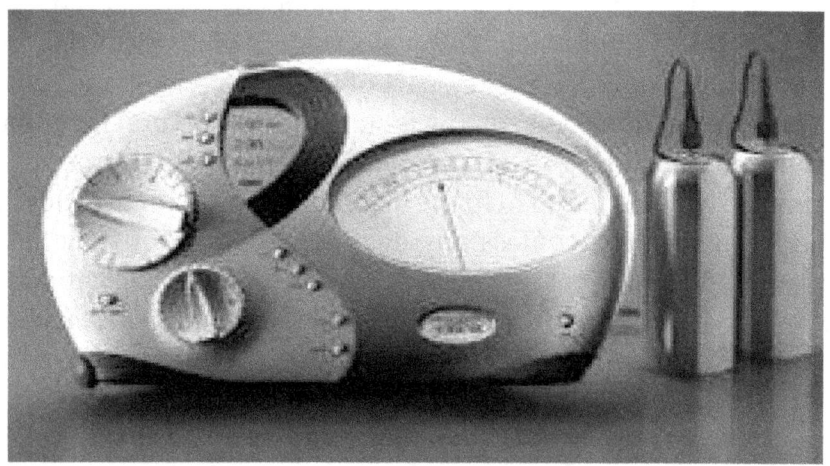

The person undergoing the audition holds an electrode, the size of a soup can, in each hand, while a flow of electricity emanating from the E-meter circulates through their body. The auditor keeps an eye on the screen while the client talks and notes every move of the needle on a sheet. These movements are supposedly triggered by the density of the electrical current flowing between the electrodes, which is purported to change in response to the client's emotions during the communication with the auditor. Stating if the person is at ease with the subject being discussed

Floating on a Pink Cloud

During one of my very first sessions, I experienced an intense, hard-to-describe phenomenon while holding the large E-meter electrodes in my hands—a sensation Scientologists refer to as a 'release.' All I had to do was hold those large electrodes that permitted the flow of electricity to circulate through my body, and suddenly, a miracle would unfold. After twenty minutes or so, I was out of my depressive state. Everything in my life felt lighter, and it felt as if I was seeing the world through a 'different filter.' Life suddenly became much more beautiful, and I was thrilled. It was like taking the perfect pill!

From that moment on, I was literally 'floating'—so much so that after a couple of auditing sessions, my auditor and the case supervisor in charge of tracking my progress decided to temporarily pause my Confessional because the needle on the E-meter screen wouldn't stop moving, due to the absence of resistance between both electrodes. A phenomenon Hubbard named a 'persistent floating needle.' They explained that in that situation, it wasn't possible to continue the process. I had to wait until I came back to earth.

Because the Confessional was mandatory, I had to commit to returning in a few days to finish the list of questions. Normally, interrupting a Confessional midway was forbidden. However, given my state, the E-meter was useless, so they allowed me to leave for my planned holiday to attend a wedding in Gaspésie. I left the day after that auditing session, during which I experienced this phenomenon. During the twelve-hour drive, sitting behind the wheel of my Chevy Cavalier, I felt on top of the world. It was as if I were floating outside my body, watching my car zoom down the highway. I drove all night, stopping only for an hour or two at dawn to try to sleep, parked by the sea. Something I couldn't do since I was so excited.

Upon arriving at the wedding venue, my euphoria intensified. The beauty of the seaside, the landscape, the feeling of freedom—all of it made the experience even more exhilarating. But soon, events started to bring me crashing down from my pink cloud. After joining in a toast to the newlyweds, I couldn't stop drinking. I had been warned in my support group not to take even a sip of alcohol. But I felt invincible being in that euphoric state. I had gradually stopped attending meetings since returning to Scientology, and I'd forgotten what life was like before I quit drinking. I thought I could handle just one sip of champagne, but it became another, and another, and on it went.

A few days later, I visited a friend in New Brunswick, where I ended up doing cocaine again. Fortunately, I only used it a few times, but each time left me in a terrible state. Still, from that point on, I began drinking far more than I had in the previous two years. When I returned to Montreal, the staff at the Church's technical division told me that my alcohol consumption wasn't an issue as long as I could abstain for 24 hours before my sessions. That was easy enough, given that I worked all day during the week and spent my evenings in the academy. Consequently, I was officially cleared to resume my Confessional sessions with the E-meter now that my needle had stopped floating. Just like me—my binge drinking and the guilt over my relapse had firmly brought me back down to Earth, and I was stressed, mostly due to the fact that I had fallen again into the pit of alcoholism.

Irrelevant Questions

During one of the early sessions, the auditor asked me personal questions about my past, such as:

> *Have you ever had sex with a member of your family?*
> *Have you ever practiced homosexuality?*

I found these particularly intrusive. I couldn't see the connection between my current disagreements with Hubbard's teachings and my past behaviors. The Johannesburg Confessional felt more like an excavation of my old sins than a corrective measure. Still, I held back my criticism, not wanting to dig myself into deeper trouble. I had no choice but to pass this test if I wanted to return to the academy and finish my courses. Determined, I convinced myself that opening up to someone and discussing my past couldn't hurt. Holding the electrodes, I answered all the questions—even those I found out of context and irrelevant, at least here in Canada:

> *Have you ever been involved in an abortion?*
> *Are you a communist?*
> *Have you ever been a member of the Communist Party?*

The questionnaire seemed outdated and pointless, and I felt it was a waste of my time at $150 an hour.

Many of these questions felt meaningless to me and clashed with my values. To make matters worse, my auditor asked if I had ever engaged in sexual intercourse with someone of color, implying it was a destructive or reprehensible act. Upon hearing that question, I was instantly offended. I had always opposed racism, viewing it as a particularly harmful flaw to human well-being! Moreover, this question clashed with Scientology's teachings, which posited that humans are primarily spiritual beings who have lived many lives, making skin color or ancestral origin secondary and insignificant. Seeing my reaction, the auditor explained that the 'Johannesburg Confessional' was named for its origins in South Africa during apartheid. At that time, having a romantic relationship with a person of color was considered immoral by many. This context, they said, was why the question had been included. I didn't argue, though I found the explanation unconvincing. Why perpetuate such absurdity? The presence of this question only reinforced prejudices and segregation. It should have been removed long ago. I realized that Hubbard's policy, prohibiting any changes—even a single comma—in his technical bulletins or on the Grade Chart, was foolish and rendered Scientology obsolete. It obstructed intellectual evolution and was detrimental to society. That day, my opinion of Hubbard had taken a significant hit.

When Doubt Sets In

During one of my subsequent auditing sessions, I was stunned when I felt a jolt of electricity from the E-meter as the auditor turned it on. Holding the electrodes, I felt the current travel up one arm, cross my neck and skull, and return down the other arm to the second electrode. It turned out the auditor had mistakenly set one of the voltage adjustment knobs incorrectly. Flabbergasted, I glanced at her and saw she was jotting something in her report. I informed her that the E-meter had given me a strong electric shock and that the needle's reaction wasn't due to my thoughts. She apologized and adjusted the knob.

I had always been fascinated by this remarkable device, which was designed to measure the emotional charge associated with specific thoughts and assess progress in confronting traumatic memories. But after this incident, my fascination with the E-meter waned considerably. I began to question its infallibility and wondered about the potential effects of the electrical current on my nervous, endocrine, or cerebral systems—and my overall health in the long run.

The Scientology organizations claimed that the E-meter measures changes in the individual's mind, but they kept quiet about the fact that it emits electricity that circulates through the body. This incident made me suspicious. As a result, the E-meter lost its mysterious allure for me, and my doubts about Scientology deepened. I started worrying since I spent hours connected to that device. However, today, I understand that the E-meter functions like a Transcutaneous Electrical Nerve Stimulation (TENS) device, having tried one of those gadgets to treat pain in my legs.

*"**Mechanisms of TENS Reduction on Analgesia** TENS activates a complex neuronal network to result in a reduction in pain. At frequencies and intensities used clinically, TENS activates large diameter afferent fibers. This afferent input is sent to the central nervous system to activate descending inhibitory systems to reduce hyperalgesia[50](...) In parallel, studies in people with fibromyalgia show that TENS can restore central pain modulation,*

a measure of central inhibition. Therefore, TENS reduces hyperalgesia through both peripheral and central mechanisms." [51]

I made the connection when I felt the same electrical flow from the TENS device, which stimulates endorphin production and acts as a painkiller. The flow was slightly more intense than what I'd felt from the E-meter, likely due to the size of the electrodes. The electrodes of the E-meter are significantly larger, spreading the electricity over a larger area of the skin and affecting a greater number of nerve terminations.

"**How TENS Units Can Help Treat Depression** *The TENS units produce sensations which help create more of a balance. Endorphins are created, along with other chemicals which help reduce the depression. This is* **especially useful for** *people who have been suffering with* **chronic depression***. It is something that you can eventually do on your own in the home environment. There are certain parts of the body that this can be more effective; for example, it can work well when the electrodes are placed on the hands as well as around the heart".* [52]

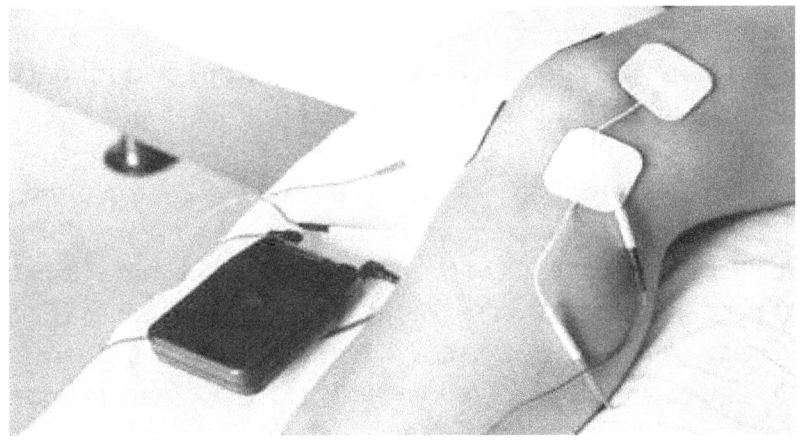

"**Understanding TENS and its Potential for Anxiety Management** *TENS, short for Transcutaneous Electrical Nerve Stimulation, is a therapy that has been used for decades to manage pain and various other conditions.*

Recently, its potential for anxiety relief has caught the attention of researchers and individuals alike. TENS involves the use of a small, battery-operated device that delivers mild electrical impulses through electrodes placed on the skin. (...) As the search for effective anxiety management techniques continues, TENS has emerged as a promising option." [53]

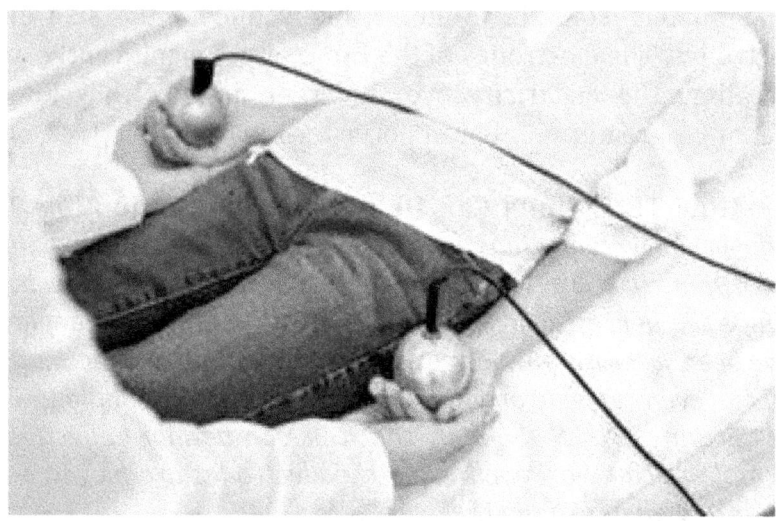

While researching online, I found that I wasn't the first to make this observation. Arnie Lerma, one of the early activists who exposed many of Hubbard's tricks, made the same claim about the E-meter on his website in 1999:

"There are various devices on the market, all licensed for use by the FDA under the direction of a physician, which consist of two electrodes which are applied to various parts of the body, as in the treatment of lower back pain. These are called TENS units TENS is an acronym for transient electro-neural stimulation. There are many flavors of these devices, including devices that have been clinically shown to provide pain relief from the effects of the electrical currents they put through your body."[54]

One of Hubbard's sons, who later changed his name to Ronald DeWolf, also talked about his father's use of 'electrical hypnosis' in one of the interviews he gave, denouncing his father. Given what I know now about Hubbard—a con man, fraudster, and drug addict who even referred to himself as the Antichrist—it's clear to me that he introduced the E-meter as a tool to trick Scientologists.

"**Scientists use high-tech brain stimulation to make people more hypnotizable.** *Stanford Medicine scientists used transcranial magnetic stimulation to temporarily enhance hypnotizability in patients with chronic pain,*
making them better candidates for hypnotherapy. (...) The researchers found that participants who received the neurostimulation showed a statistically significant increase in hypnotizability, scoring roughly one point higher. The sham group experienced no effect." [55]

CHAPTER 17

A BREACH OF CONFIDENTIALITY

Another incident that occurred during my Johannesburg Confessional sessions made me question the professionalism of the church and the conduct of certain staff members. As a result, I began to lose faith in the therapeutic process I was supposed to benefit from during my time in Scientology. At the time, I was dating a woman named Sophie, whom I had met at the Montreal organization. Our romantic relationship was blossoming, and I had grown to like her a lot.

However, one evening, while we were having dinner at a restaurant, she asked me a personal question—something from my ethics file. She wanted to know if what she'd heard about my past was true. Instead of answering, I asked her where she'd gotten that information. Hesitantly, she confessed it had come from a former ethics officer at the Montreal organization, someone she was close to. She admitted he had shared this strictly confidential information with her during a private conversation.

I remember meeting this guy in the ethics officer's office a few weeks earlier after he'd received a Knowledge Report about me from another Scientologist I knew back when I was still using. That day, I had to convince him that I'd changed my ways—that I was in Scientology because I genuinely wanted to become a better person. Unfortunately, after I got angry that evening, Sophie stopped seeing me.

Frustrated, I brought it up during my next auditing session. I reported the breach to my auditor, but nothing was done, and that man went unpunished. I even crossed the guy twice in the organization! Seeing no action taken, I lost faith in the organization. I realized then that everything I shared in those 'excavation' sessions was documented, and anyone with access to the files could use it against me. I thought about all the people who had served as ethics officers over the years, including one individual with a serious criminal record who became an ethics officer the same year he was released from prison. Honestly, almost any staff member had access to everyone's ethics file. Confidentiality is non-existent in Scientology. There is no redemption in that so-called 'church!'

The PTS/SP Course

The second course in the famous three-pack, for which I never got reimbursed, was called the PTS/SP Course. In this course, we explored the twelve characteristics of a Suppressive Person, learning how to identify these individuals who are considered 'to be avoided at all costs.' Since Hubbard told us that man was fundamentally good, he used the course to explain how someone could end up becoming suppressive.

It wasn't about analyzing or reflecting on oppression. My job was to absorb the material and memorize each characteristic so I could spot a Suppressive Person. Hubbard also taught us how to recognize a PTS (Potential Trouble Source) and help them escape their condition. The solution? Find the SP in their life—usually someone antagonistic to Scientology—and either disconnect from them or, if that wasn't possible, avoid triggering conversations.

There was no room for doubt. Comparing Hubbard's teachings with other theories was not an option while studying. Scientology, as presented by Hubbard, was perfect. Even considering improvements was a major crime. Hubbard was the sole credible source, and all we had to do was internalize his word. I also had to memorize the Tone Scale. Sitting in a chair facing a wall with a poster of the scale, I repeated each tone and its corresponding number until I could recite the entire sequence by heart to the course supervisor—that's when I earned my 'pass.'

In this course, Hubbard also shared the types of individuals to avoid. This included homosexuals, whom he labeled as perverse and dangerous, stuck at 1.1 on the Tone Scale under 'Covered Hostility.' Journalists, whom he called "merchants of chaos," were another group to be avoided. And, of course, anyone with a profession starting with 'psych.' People who were antagonistic toward Scientology were also automatically classified as suppressive. In the end, it seemed like I was being told to avoid a whole lot of people!

The third and final course in the pack, Upper Indoctrination TRs, involved several TRs that had to be practiced with another Scientologist in the same course, but there wasn't anyone available. While waiting for someone to enroll, I decided to try the Purification Rundown. I figured it might help since the program was designed to detoxify the body by sweating out toxins or drugs supposedly stuck in body fat. It was all done in a sauna, and the Rundown promised to restore vitality and clear the mind, just as the title of the book I had to read beforehand suggested: Clear Body, Clear Mind.

Physical danger

I paid an additional $1,500 for the Purification Rundown, which was supposed to last approximately a month. By now, I'd spent roughly $8,000 in just over a year. That was quite a bit for someone in my financial situation at the time, although it was a drop in the ocean compared to what other Scientologists were investing 'for their future and the future of humanity.' Once again, I wondered why authorities hadn't at least required the Church of Scientology to inform clients about the potential risks of this program. They'd received warnings about the dangers of the Purification Rundown. Was it all in the name of religious freedom? Or did some Scientologists hold positions of power in the government?

After a few weeks of this treatment, I began suffering from terrible discomfort and heat strokes, which triggered a new state of dissociation. Of course, I chalked the emotional release I was experiencing up to Hubbard's 'miraculous technology.' Hubbard, probably inspired by Indigenous sweat lodges used in shamanic ceremonies, had simply found another way to induce that same state in Scientologists! Luckily, as far as I know, no deaths in Canada have been directly linked to the Purification Rundown. Sadly, it seems the authorities may be waiting for that to happen before taking action.

In July 2011, a thirty-five-year-old Quebec mother named Gabriel Lavigne lost her life in a sweat ritual similar to the one Hubbard designed. In this personal development seminar, participants were covered in mud, wrapped in sheets, and then encased in plastic wrap and three blankets. They were left in this state for almost nine hours, their heads covered with cardboard boxes. Madam Lavigne was literally cooked to death by the seminar's organizer, Gabrielle Fréchette, who called herself 'Serena' and claimed to be possessed by an energy entity named 'Melkisédeck.' She served three years in prison for criminal negligence. Her assistant received two years.

In another incident, this one in the mystical red cliffs of Sedona, Arizona, three people died during a sweat lodge ritual at an 'enlightenment seminar' led by New Age guru James Arthur Ray. He was convicted for the deaths that occurred in October 2009.

> *"Cults start seducing people with love-bombing, paying a great deal of attention to and being very affectionate with potential recruits. A very effective way of connecting with someone who is feeling lonely and isolated. Then, they assault and overwhelm their senses by using various techniques to induce a dissociated state, an altered state of consciousness, a trance state in which mind and body are disconnected from each other. These techniques include sleep and food deprivation, drumming, chanting, lecturing on and on for hours, flashing lights, spinning around in circles, all of which assault the senses and break down a person's ability to think. The cult uses mind control to fill the dissociated mind with their beliefs and magical thinking."*[56]   Sharon K. Farber

The Purification Rundown is a required step at the beginning of the Bridge. No wonder why, since it is so effective in putting people in a dissociative state!

Freedom of religion

As a Scientologist, I always felt I had to contribute to 'saving the planet.' However, since I had struggled before regaining some control over my finances after getting clean and sober in the fall of 1993, my financial resources were limited. Over the span of two years, I bought a package of three major courses, paid for the confessional, and completed the Purification Rundown. I'd also spent a few thousand more to become a lifetime member of the *International Association of Scientologists*. So, at that point, I felt I had contributed enough financially and decided to stop giving money to Scientology if I wanted to keep my credit intact.

However, despite my financial difficulties, I remained committed to defending the concept of 'freedom of religion.' Although I had sworn off ever returning to the Sea Org, the 'Johnny Goodboy' in me wasn't completely dead. I regularly took part in demonstrations in Montreal, Quebec City, and Toronto to support the Church of Scientology's battles. I also actively participated in anti-psychiatry protests organized by the Citizens' Commission on Human Rights (CCHR), a group affiliated with Scientology, which opposes psychiatry. When in 1995, Scientology's top brass called on all its organizations worldwide to send representatives to Frankfurt, Germany, for a 'call to arms' in response to legal actions taken against the church in that country. I volunteered to go to Europe, even though I had no more money. I managed to be sponsored by other Scientologists, who covered my plane ticket and lodging while I took care of the rest. Two of us from the Montreal organization traveled to Europe to join this grand march for religious freedom.

To keep costs low, my fellow Scientologist and I opted to stay at a youth hostel. The next day, we met a group of Scientologists from Italy and left with them to the rally point. There, the march organizers were waiting to give us instructions on how to proceed. We were instructed to remain peaceful and united to ensure the demonstration's success. Afterward, we'd be taken by bus to a place where we could eat and drink. After hours of marching through the streets of Frankfurt, we finally boarded the buses, excited to sit down and relax. But, to my surprise, as I looked out the window to catch a glimpse of the country I'd never visited, I realized we were headed to an industrial area. We were taken to the backyard of some factory, a rather bleak setting where a small stage had been set up, and rows of chairs had been arranged in front of it. Thinking it was a wrap-up conference, I sat down—only to discover that we had been brought here for a fundraiser for the International Association of Scientologists.

International Association of Scientologists

I always believed that the money raised at these events was supposed to fund efforts to reduce drug use and crime, help kids in need, or support battered women around the world, all through the Church of However, the funds are actually kept in a holding account located in Curaçao, a tax haven, and are entirely separate from the Church itself. These funds are at the disposal of senior Church leaders, who can use them however they see fit. They might finance expensive ad campaigns, like the ones shown during the Super Bowl, or build luxurious guesthouses on Scientology compounds to host VIPs like Tom Cruise or John Travolta when they visit. They're also used to pay private investigators to follow and harass ex-members who speak out or to cover legal fees for the Church's many court cases worldwide.

I later learned that a significant portion of the funds raised went directly into the pockets of the event hosts and organizers. I, on the other hand, often maxed out my credit cards at these fundraisers, where everyone was encouraged to 'do their part.' But at this point in my life, I promised myself that I wouldn't let it happen again. At these events, participants challenge one another through games, competing to outdo each other in pledges and reach the fundraising goal set for the evening—sometimes exceeding hundreds of thousands of dollars. I had distanced myself from the association because I had never seen any campaigns that truly worked to improve humanity, at least not ones directly funded by the association. I felt that we were being blatantly misled when they claimed that the money was going to projects aimed at improving society and humanity.

Yet, there I was, stuck in one of these events against my will, in the middle of an industrial neighborhood in a city I didn't know, in a country where I wasn't exactly welcomed as a Scientologist, and where I didn't even speak the language. Feeling utterly betrayed, I got up from my seat and waited by the buses to return to town—which didn't happen for several hours!

According to Scientology researcher Jeffrey Augustine, the International Association of Scientologists is an autonomous entity separate from the Church, holding, in 2017, nearly $1.5 billion in liquid assets. Meanwhile, the Church of Scientology is estimated to be worth around $1.7 billion, with a majority of its assets invested in real estate.

CHAPTER 18

UPPER INDOCTRINATION

After returning from Germany, I continued visiting Montreal's Scientology organization for a while. I'd to complete the courses I'd started to avoid ending up in the ethics department. Although increasingly disgusted by the behavior of certain Scientologists, I remained committed to completing the last course, which primarily involved TRs and was the second step after the Purification Rundown on the path to Clear. Even though achieving that state of Clear wasn't a personal goal, I still hoped to find something liberating in the process. That course, which mainly consisted of auditing processes under the form of TRs, was done by co-auditing with
a 'twin' who was at the same level as me.

To start, we had to refine TRs 0 to 4, which we had already practiced in the Communication Course. Thankfully, they had become much easier to master this time. I almost automatically entered the light state of dissociation required to do them. The main difference with the TRs done in the Communication Course was that we now had to remain in control of the TRs for much longer. We spent much more time on each exercise, acquiring an advanced level of 'communication control' to deliver auditing to our twin.

Once again, I spent several hours on each stage of TR 0. By then, I could remain utterly detached from my emotions, showing no reaction to insults, jokes, or the various comical, derogatory, and offensive remarks my twin hurled at me. Through TRs 1 to 4, as seen in the Communication Course, I practiced controlling communication from different angles. In one TR, I had to ensure my twin always responded to my commands. In another, I had to acknowledge their questions so thoroughly that they felt heard and no longer needed to keep talking.

In this course, we were introduced to TRs 5 to 9. These were openly presented as auditing processes, though it felt odd since we were training to control bodies. However, I quickly understood why they were considered 'therapeutic' when I experienced extreme dissociation again during one of these exercises.

In TR 5, where we practiced standing, I had to consider my twin as a spiritual entity—a thetan in Scientology jargon—separate from his body. While doing the TR, I would address my commands to the thetan, starting with: "*Sit this body on this chair.*" My twin would pretend to resist or want to leave the session, and I had to persistently order the thetan to sit the body down until I demonstrated that I had the skill to convince a thetan to obey. As with all TRs, my twin would then practice controlling me in turn, treating me as a thetan. I'd either refuse or comply with the instruction to sit my body on a chair.

In the next exercise, keeping in mind that I was a thetan, controlling a body, I had to grab my twin's arm and physically direct it in a chosen direction as though it were my own body. Then, I'd stop the movement, start again, and maintain control over my twin's body. Sometimes, my twin would resist slightly to make sure I could control the body. Throughout the drill, I had to treat my twin as a thetan when speaking to him. Hubbard instructed us, through his material, to use the highest levels of the Tone Scale when addressing the thetan. I did my best to operate at levels such as Action, Games, Postulates, and, ideally, the Serenity of Being, avoiding the lower emotions at all costs.

Scientology "Exteriorization"

At a certain point in the exercise, thanks to various factors—like the cheerful attitude needed for adopting an elevated and serene tone, the ongoing practice of TR 0, the idea that I was a thetan addressing another thetan, and the exhausting repetition of the exercise that lasted several hours—I began to genuinely believe I was outside my body. From then on, I used the physical universe merely to transmit vocal commands to my twin. The mundane exercise of control suddenly transformed into a powerful process. At that moment, I felt as if I was floating a meter above my body, experiencing the same euphoric sensation I had felt before. I then told my twin that I no longer felt the need to exist in the physical universe and that I felt like a powerful spiritual being, not just the pile of flesh I was dragging around. My twin ended the session for the evening and reported it to the case supervisor. As had happened at the beginning of my Confessional, I was removed from the course because I was deemed too high to continue. I told the case supervisor that I had achieved a significant win during the auditing process and felt I had completed that step on the Bridge.

'Low-Level' Marines

Around 1997, an event made me question my admiration for the Sea Org members. That summer, administrators came from Flag Land Base on a mission to sell higher-level auditing services, which were only available in advanced organizations. Nostalgic for the days when I vowed to work for the protection of humanity; I wanted to help them. Although I couldn't make the countless sacrifices required by being in the Sea Org, I still wanted to show respect for those who had devoted their lives to the cause. So, I made myself available.

Before long, I found myself behind the wheel of my car with one of these guys beside me—someone I considered a bit of a marine. He asked me to drive him around Montreal because he needed to find something for his superior, a woman in her fifties who was also a Sea Org member and responsible for the mission. This woman had demanded that her colleague, obviously under her orders, find her some of those raw sausages called Gendarme, to which she was addicted. During the drive, my companion, around forty years old, told me he often found himself in this situation, spending hours searching for these sausages in unfamiliar towns to satisfy his superior's cravings. I was shocked and disappointed by this woman's behavior. She was using the Sea Org's human resources to fulfill her gluttony, turning this man into an ordinary 'sausage hunter.' To me, it made no sense. I realized that the Sea Org was nothing like the elite I once thought it was.

In addition to helping these members, I spent a lot of time in the academy assisting students with the E-meter. I held the electrodes while they asked questions and observed the device's dial. I could spend entire evenings holding the electrodes without paying attention to the electrical current circulating through my body.

As luck would have it, during this period, I began to experience the same euphoria I had felt during my Johannesburg Confessional. It became unpleasant since I found myself in this state at 10:30 p.m., knowing I had to go to sleep so I could get up for work the next morning. I resorted to drinking a few beers to relax and get some sleep. Luckily, I avoided drugs because I couldn't imagine what might have happened if I had consumed them, being in that state! I should have stopped holding the electrodes for other students, but at that time, I didn't know it was putting me in that state. And I had nothing else to do but spend my evening at the Scientology org.

As my twenty-fifth birthday approached, I was trying to regain control of my life. I clung to Scientology, which was almost the only stable thing around me, all I had left of a social life. I attended all the promotional events organized by the Montreal Church of Scientology since I enjoyed dressing up and meeting other Scientologists. Events celebrating Hubbard's birthday, the first publication of Dianetics, and so on. They also launched new Scientology breakthroughs and primarily served to sell books and courses or raise money for the Church, but I wasn't interested in it. I got into the habit of leaving early to avoid the hard-sell tactics the staff used to try to sell them or book appointments. At that time, I wrote this text in French, which came to me out of nowhere while I was strumming my guitar:

Since the dawn of time, in the drizzle and in the wind,
I have been looking for you
I was told of a path that leads to your wisdom
Reveal it to me; show me that path to find you."

Through this text, I admitted to myself that my search for meaning was still very much alive and that Scientology wasn't providing the nourishment I needed. I wasn't going to find answers to the questions that had begun surfacing the day I fell to my knees on Denise's balcony in Scientology. Consequently, I realized that if I had to pursue a spiritual journey, it would be somewhere else, as Scientology was totalitarian and left no room for other beliefs. In the weeks that followed, I stopped attending the Montreal organization's academy, feeling disinterested and confused. By not starting a new course, I managed to avoid the ethics officer for having 'blown,' which allowed me to stay on good terms with the Church of Scientology— a priority for me since I didn't want to cut ties with my loved ones who were in Scientology. I had found new, less restrictive ways to spend my evenings.

Around that time, I began singing country and retro music in various city bars, particularly at 'La Boussole,' a cabaret on Mont-Royal Street, just a short walk from the Scientology organization and my home. Access to a microphone was all I needed to be happy! By day, I worked in a factory, and by night, I practiced music. On weekends, I sang at the cabaret with my new friend Fernand, who played the keyboard. However, spending more and more time in bars led to increased drinking for me. Often, I ended my evenings alone, falling asleep on my sofa in front of the television with a glass of red wine in hand or with any woman willing to tolerate my drunken state.

On Monday mornings, I would drag myself out of bed at the last minute and head to a job I had come to despise. I continued working as a metal tool worker, a trade I had learned at the Juvenile Center, which paid well despite my intense need for human contact and intellectual stimulation. Burdened with debt, depleted savings, and no borrowing capacity due to my investments in Scientology, I couldn't afford to quit that job. So, I remained in the factory for forty-five to fifty hours a week, counting down the days until the weekend came. Only alcohol and, above all, music, which fascinated me more each day, kept me relatively content.

However, professional burnout eventually took its toll. One morning, I couldn't get up from my bed. To cope, I started taking various natural supplements, including large doses of liquid vitamin C provided by a naturopath friend who had moved in with me. Then, the situation worsened when I lost my driver's license for drinking and driving. Because of that, I had to leave home even earlier to commute to work by public transport. One morning, after getting off the bus, I broke down in tears as I walked the few streets to the metal shop. That day, I sank back into despair and realized that my exhaustion stemmed partly from hating my job.

By chance, a conflict with a Jehovah's Witness prompted me to leave the factory job. This coworker, who had been trying to bring to his religious meetings since we met, had recently begun criticizing Scientology, which shocked me. Given his own controversial beliefs and our supposed mutual support in the name of 'freedom of religion,' his attacks on Scientology were unacceptable. I decided he was a suppressive person and avoided him, leading to my departure from the job.

After leaving the factory, I took time to recover from my burnout and eventually decided to apply to McGill University's Faculty of Music. My growing passion for classical singing, theater, and opera gave me hope. A few months later, I auditioned for the classical singing program and returned home feeling cautiously optimistic. In the following month, I receive a letter from McGill University. Feverishly, I opened it and learned that I was accepted as a mature student in the general music program for classical singing. I had never been so happy and proud, especially considering my disastrous educational background.

Music as a Refuge

The acceptance was a beacon of light, pulling me out of the darkness I had fallen into in the last months. That summer, I eagerly awaited the fall session. Even before classes began, I spent my days in the Faculty of Music's practice rooms and library. I loved those buildings and could easily spend entire days at the piano or vocalizing. Then, the session started: Music theory, solfeggio, music history, ear training, private singing lessons with a renowned teacher, and other classes filled my schedule. I was on cloud nine! Studying full-time in a music faculty felt like a dream come true. It gave me confidence in myself and my 'destiny.' For the first time, I truly felt privileged.

At McGill, I sang in several choirs and even got a leading role in an operetta. I attended countless concerts, immersing myself in classical music and dramatic opera. This passion, rooted in my childhood with Geneviève, allowed me to gradually distance myself from Scientology and fully invest in my new life.

However, my feeling of superiority couldn't mask my lack of self-confidence or the nagging sense of being an impostor. As in the Juvenile center, I often felt apart from others. I was still embarrassed by my first name and would arrive early to each class, asking the professor to add 'Michel' before Laflèche on the attendance list. I even called the Director of Civil Status before university to inquire about officially changing my first name, but the process was so complicated and expensive that I gave up.

Of course, I attended first-year student parties. However, I should've avoided heavy drinking, knowing full well that alcohol was an issue for me. Eventually, I also began using marijuana again. The first time I smoked, after nearly five years without any drugs, I immediately felt like a fog of depression lifted. For a time, I started smoking small joints, just like my father had. I was trying to self-medicate, but the grass I found was too strong, and again, I became paranoiac as I had been before quitting in 1993 when I left Denise. So, I mostly drank. I could more easily control my consumption of alcohol, and since it was socially acceptable, even though the drinking distracted me from my studies, with almost no formal background in classical music and a chaotic academic history, I should have focused much more on practicing.

Meanwhile, the Montreal Scientology organization continued demanding my involvement and financial sacrifices. However, as my skepticism toward Hubbard's teachings grew, I gradually pulled away. I think they sensed my priorities had shifted when I firmly declined the Director of the Office of Special Affairs request to leverage any government contacts I had for lobbying efforts. I told him I wouldn't participate and that if Scientology had any real merit, it would stand the test of time without such tactics. I wasn't putting any more effort into it.

To Dare

One afternoon around the year 2000, while searching for a document at a municipal library, I stumbled upon an unauthorized biography of L. Ron Hubbard titled Bare-Faced Messiah. This book, written by journalist Russell Miller, was the result of years of investigation and had been well- received by the English press. Against the advice of my former 'guru,' I dared to read it. As I worked my way through the pages, I was confronted with the true story of Scientology's founder. The author questioned nearly the entire image Hubbard had carefully crafted, which was carried by Scientology organizations. Miller portrayed Hubbard as a charismatic, convincing mythomaniac who managed to deceive countless people. Reading this book opened my eyes and forced me to question my involvement with Scientology. It felt like a veil had been lifted, revealing the cracks in a foundation I had once believed unshakable. The more I learned about Hubbard's life, the more disillusioned I became with the organization I had devoted so much of my time and energy to.

CHAPTER 19

WIND OF CHANGE

From the day I finished reading Russell Miller's book, the doubt that had crept into my mind years earlier solidified into a strong negative opinion toward Scientology. I began to see its teachings and founder in a completely different light. At my father's insistence, I attended a few events organized by the Church, although only when they took place outside Montreal's organizational building. However, I stopped going after noticing blatant lies in a film about L. Ron Hubbard's life, which was projected on a giant screen on his birthday. They were in complete contradiction with Miller's affirmation, and I knew the facts presented by the BBC journalist in Bare-Faced Messiah were accurate. I understood that the Church of Scientology was literally lying to us.

As for my music studies, while my initial time at McGill's Faculty of Music felt like a fairy tale, I quickly realized I couldn't keep up with the intensive program. It went beyond simple misunderstandings of texts and stemmed from deeper personal issues. My father, to whom I confided about my struggles, saw me as a traitor for joining what he called the 'enemy camp.' In his eyes, McGill was the cradle of psychiatry in North America, and he had hoped that one of his children would attend a university, yet now he resented it.

I was trying my hardest to succeed, but I had serious problems focusing during solfeggio and ear training. Worse, I didn't know how to write a term paper, having never done that kind of writing before, and my lack of a solid academic background weighed heavily on me. Since I couldn't manage to work much while studying full-time, I struggled financially. As I feared my dream slipping away, I sought help from McGill's Student Support Department. This eventually led me to a psychiatrist's office, hoping to avoid getting kicked out of university.

I'll never forget the day I climbed the steps of the mental health clinic. I was nearly shaking at the thought of entering a psychiatrist's office. I hesitated, a flood of questions racing through my mind. Was I about to do something irreparable, something that would endanger my spiritual freedom forever, just as Scientology had warned? Should I tell the psych I had spent years in Scientology and that I was once their worst enemy? That I had protested against psychiatry, standing on the front lines of demonstrations? If I walked through that door, would I come out unscathed, or would they lock me up in a hospital? Would they strap me to a bed, force pills down my throat, and lobotomize me because I had once opposed them?

I knew one thing for sure—I could never go back to the Church of Scientology and admit that I had seen a psychiatrist. Hubbard's writings were clear: Psychiatry was the ultimate enemy. If I did this, I'd be crucified alive by the Ethics department. I was at a crossroads, and I decided to follow my dreams, not Hubbard's directives. I had already sacrificed enough—money, time, and sanity—without real success. I wasn't about to sacrifice my music dream, too. Finally, I walked into the clinic and was greeted by a warm woman in her early thirties. She smiled kindly and invited me to sit in her office. Her voice was gentle, and I immediately felt more at ease. She asked what brought me there, and I relaxed, opening up about my struggles and how powerless I felt in the face of my academic challenges. To my surprise, she expressed admiration for how far I had come. She said the fact that I was in university and talking to her about it was a testament to my strength. I had faced so many obstacles, yet here I was. Her words were filled with empathy and compassion, qualities I'd never experienced in Scientology.

I also tried to explain the strange phenomenon I had experienced during my Scientology TRs—the detachment and calm that would wash over me due to dissociation. But she didn't understand since I didn't know the right words at that time. I mimicked the expressions from the Tone Scale poster, hoping to explain, but it didn't translate. Disappointed, I gave up, worried she'd think I was crazy. Still, she encouraged me to keep going. She assured me that earning my bachelor's degree would boost my self-confidence and serve as a springboard for future achievements. She mentioned medication as an option for what might be an attention disorder, but when she saw my reaction, she quickly dropped the idea and let me go without pushing it.

In the days that followed, I often thought about my meeting with her. Talking with that psychiatrist had done me a world of good. In just an hour, I had received more warmth and humanity than I had ever experienced in Scientology. But I didn't return. For me, going to see her had been a monumental step—I had finally confronted the 'enemy' and seen that psychiatrists weren't monsters. Clinging to my dream, I applied for admission to the University of Quebec in Montreal (UQAM) for a music program. The teaching was in French, and the level was lower, which I hoped would make things easier for me.

A Different University

At UQAM, I participated in several musical productions, particularly the opera workshop, and it made me happy. But academically, I didn't fare much better than I had at McGill, and my social life was bleak. I often found myself alone, being a little older than the average student, and I had completely stopped going to the Scientology organization in Montreal.

During one of my last trimesters at UQAM, the September 11, 2001, terrorist attack happened. That day, it was all over the television screens at the university. I was shocked. It felt like I had to pull my head out of the comfortable cocoon of the music faculty and face the harsh reality of the world. Around the same time, a young pianist I worked with on my songs—a woman in her early twenties—took her own life. That was too much for me to handle.

Feeling isolated, facing failure, and watching my dream of a music career slip away, I found myself in a spiral of distress. The truth became clear: I wouldn't be able to finish my bachelor's degree. The courses I'd taken in Scientology, which were supposed to help me, had been useless. I wasn't some 'above average' thetan. In fact, I was struggling in every aspect of my life. By the beginning of 2003, I had stopped attending UQAM altogether.

After quitting my music studies, I sought solace in bars and drinking, and for a while, it worked. But in the fall of 2003, an incident occurred that made me realize I could no longer take refuge in alcohol. One Saturday evening, at closing time in a brasserie on the Plateau-Mont-Royal, I was overcome by an unbearable thirst. It brought out traits in me I had never expressed before. That evening, determined to keep drinking even though the waitress had stopped serving me because it was closing time, I got up and poured myself a glass of beer from a full pitcher that another customer had ordered just before the 'last call.' I insisted, practically demanding the guy let me have it, and seeing how aggressive I was becoming, he finally gave in. With a mix of pity and disdain, he refilled my glass, calling me a loser in the process. Shocked by his comment, I snapped and pushed him. He fell off his bench, taking his beer with him, which shattered on the floor.

The waitress, who had witnessed everything, grabbed my hand as if I were a misbehaving child and led me to the door. She told me I needed help and that I was no longer welcome in her establishment. Humiliated, I went home that night without getting that final beer. The next day, still reeling from the shame, I decided it was time to go back to a meeting for alcoholics and drug addicts, as I had done a few times before. That day, I finally found my way back to sobriety.

Narconon

At the start of this new phase of abstinence from all drugs and alcohol, I got involved with Narconon, a satellite of the Church of Scientology that spread Hubbard's teachings as a treatment for alcoholics and drug addicts. While I didn't see Scientology as a religion, I thought maybe Hubbard's teachings could help others like me. Plus, I figured I'd improve my own chances by helping people escape the hell of addiction.

To raise funds for Narconon, I wrote and recorded on a CD, a song in English that I thought I could sell. Looking back at the lyrics, it was clear I was describing what Scientologists call 'exteriorization,' which is really just extreme dissociation—that modified state of consciousness you could also call a hypnotic trance. Detached from my negative emotions and my suffering, thanks to Hubbard's 'miraculous technology,' I expressed in my song, how I managed to see my life in a whole new way.

Life Reaches High
On a day that I will never forget, I was there, sitting all on my own.
Full of pain, emptiness, and regrets Wishing people would leave me alone
I was searching for a way to the stars, to a place where I could finally win
I was searching for a way to the stars When they showed me how to spread my wings
Life Reaches Heights Life Reaches Heights Life Reaches Heights, and now I'm living this life as a king
Yesterday, I was looking around, at myself from this new point of view
What I saw was a man with a crown What I saw was the man that I knew.

Scientology had me soaring so high out of my depressive state. I felt like a king, looking at my life from a dissociated state, imagining that I was the person I had dreamed of becoming as a child!

Since I knew Narconon clients practiced TRs and did the Purification Rundown, I believed they were likely to experience the same phenomena I had encountered at the org in Montreal. At the time, I thought that was a good thing. However, what I didn't realize was that using this kind of technique compulsively to induce trance states could trigger mental disorders in vulnerable people—like drug addicts, for example. Constantly trying to dissociate from your emotions can put you at risk of developing depersonalization disorders.

I spent a few months at Narconon in Montreal and Trois-Rivières, feeling at home among the Scientologists on staff. But soon enough, I had to admit to myself that if Hubbard's technology hadn't helped me stay sober long-term, it wasn't going to do much more for Narconon's clients. I admitted it was my regular attendance at support groups that had truly helped me find lasting sobriety. Scientology had nothing to do with it.

So, I returned to my meetings and started paying more attention. I'd hear about prayer, meditation, and introspection—practices encouraged in these groups for anyone seeking lasting sobriety. Meditation, in particular, caught my interest. I'd heard about it before, always in glowing terms. One of my uncles had been practicing Transcendental Meditation regularly since he left The Mission. I'd tried bringing it up with other addicts, but I couldn't quite grasp the concept. That's when I started thinking that taking a meditation class might be the best way to learn more.

That's how I ended up attending a meditation class with Dorothée, a woman I had noticed during my first attempt at sobriety ten years earlier and was now in a relationship with. I happily accepted her invitation to join her on a Wednesday evening in the fall of 2005 for a free meditation session at Centre L'Émergence, located in a building on Saint-Denis Street in Montreal.

Chapter 20

Meditation in the Brahma Kumaris' Style

For my first meditation experience, I accompanied Dorothée to a free lesson at a center she had recently started frequenting. We arrived a few minutes early. Dorothée, familiar with the place, led me to a room behind the reception area. It was a small room with a few rows of chairs facing a little stage. In the middle of the platform was a padded armchair. Above it, hanging on the wall, was an orange poster, and in the center of the poster was a dot that shimmered like a diamond under the lights.

Once inside, Dorothée sat down toward the back, wrapping herself in a white shawl, and motioned for me to sit beside her. I was relieved I didn't have to sit in the lotus position. Before starting to meditate, I took a moment to take in my surroundings. A few others were present, nearly all dressed in white, silently staring at the shimmering dot a few feet in front of them. On the wall were portraits of a man and a woman who appeared to be from Hindu. Pakistanis or Bangladeshi origin.

Seeing these two figures dressed in white like the others, I realized I was in some sort of temple—not just a meditation center. This didn't exactly reassure me. I wasn't looking for a guru; I just wanted to learn how to meditate. Still, I decided to stay for Dorothée's sake and not leave her stranded. Without overthinking the status of these individuals, I began staring at the glittering dot on the poster, as suggested. Sitting in my chair, I instinctively adopted the posture I had often taken during TRs at Scientology academies. I focused on this imitation of a sparkling diamond projected by the lights. My gaze soon locked onto the dot about twenty feet away, and my vision blurred before sharpening again, with that single point becoming my sole focus. After about twenty minutes of this routine, I felt a mild sense of detachment and abandonment—similar to what I'd experienced during TR 0, though much less intense. Perhaps because this time, I didn't have to stare into anyone's eyes. And then, the class was over.

A Great 'Spiritual Journey'

Curious after attending a few free meditation sessions, I told Dorothée I wanted to learn more about meditation and the Brahma Kumaris. She didn't seem surprised by my request. Dorothée believed I already had a solid 'spiritual journey,' given my long involvement in Scientology (though she knew nothing about it). She invited me to join her for the level one course, which was starting a few days later, even though I hadn't formally met with anyone from the center for approval. According to her, my participation shouldn't be a problem.

Entering my first Level One lesson, I was pleased to recognize the woman who would be teaching the meditation course. She had been born into the Mission of the Holy Spirit a few years before me, and she knew who I was, as Dorothée had already mentioned me. I greeted her with my brightest smile, but she seemed less than thrilled by my presence— maybe because I hadn't officially registered and didn't have the necessary prerequisites. However, Dorothée had spoken to my father's cousin and personally invited me, assuring her there was no issue with my participation. Thanks to her, I was allowed to join the class. Slightly embarrassed, I promised to be attentive and eager to learn more about meditation.

"You must fix your sight on the point located in the center of the poster, imagining that it is God. Do this while repeating to yourself the following sentence: I am a spiritual being. In this way, you will become aware of your spiritual nature and establish a link with the

supreme soul, which will purify you by ridding you of many layers of impurity you have accumulated over your incarnations. As a jeweler would do when cutting a rough diamond, to make it pure."

That's what the teacher told us, sitting in the chair on the platform, as she pointed to the sparkling point at the center of the poster hanging on the wall behind her. It was a type of speech I was already familiar with since, as Dorothée often said, "I was no novice in matters of spirituality."

In Scientology, I'd learned the same principle when I was twelve: that we were spirits experiencing multiple reincarnations in bodies. And from my earliest childhood, I'd been made to understand that I was unworthy, branded as a 'child of Satan.' All these ideas just kept resurfacing, only dressed up in different terms.

The teacher then suggested we join her in a short period of meditation. I quickly got to work, repeating the phrase, "I am a spiritual being," while staring at the diamond in front of me. But I soon realized there was no point in repeating it—I had long since absorbed this belief. Still, I kept my focus on the little diamond and slipped into a slight hypnotic trance.

I relaxed, letting go of the negative emotions I'd felt when meeting the teacher, who, as it turned out, was my father's cousin. I allowed the stress of the day to melt away. Still, I stayed on guard—something told me that this place wasn't just a simple 'school' of meditation. That concerned me. The last thing I wanted was to get entangled in another new religious movement like Scientology.

After a brief meditation, the teacher resumed her speech. She introduced herself as a Brahmin and explained that she spent much of her time meditating to purify her karma. I listened politely, all the while analyzing her words.

"A trance is a phenomenon in which our consciousness or awareness is modified. Our awareness seems to split as our active critical evaluative thinking dims, and we slip from an active into a passive-receptive mode of mental processing. We listen or look without reflection or evaluation. We suspend rational analysis,

independent judgment, and conscious decision-making about what we are hearing or taking in."

Margaret Thaler Singer, Cults in our Midst.

An Apocalyptic Cult

Eventually, she informed us that humanity had reached the end of a 5,000-year cycle, indicating that this world, as we know it, was nearing its end. It would eventually transform into a place where only the purest beings would have the chance to reincarnate—a new world she called the 'Golden Age.' She urged us to follow her example, cleanse our karma, and earn a few extra reincarnations on this paradise-like Earth.

I listened, swallowing hard. The teacher was preaching more theology than meditation, and that did not interest me at all—quite the opposite! I felt as though I'd been duped, lured into this course with the promise of learning meditation, only to find myself in another new religious movement offering salvation for my 'fallen soul.' I wanted to get up and leave, but I didn't want to embarrass Dorothée. Since the teacher had graciously allowed me to join, I stayed and paid attention.

Then, the teacher added that bringing new children into the world was madness, given the imminent end of time, and that we should stop all sexual relations since their only purpose was procreation. I felt like she was directing this comment at Dorothée and me, especially since we were intimate, and she was trying to turn Dorothée into a Brahmin. The course wrapped up after we spent about thirty minutes staring at the glowing point. Dorothée and I left without speaking to my father's cousin—the teacher—whom I'd hoped to shake hands with and ask a few questions. She had simply vanished!

On the way home, questions buzzed in my mind about my father's cousin. Why had she reacted so coldly upon seeing me? Did she know a former Scientologist like me couldn't be convinced by the ideas she was teaching? How could she subscribe to a philosophy that advocated for the slow extinction of humanity? Was this a reaction to the Mission's teachings, which promoted repopulating the Earth by having as many consecrated children as possible? There were so many questions, and none of them have been answered to this day.

Naturally, I didn't continue the Level One courses. I couldn't subscribe to the teachings they offered in that first lesson. But I did return to L'Émergence to meditate. I enjoyed their meditation technique, which closely resembled self-hypnosis, with its prolonged fixation on the diamond at the center of the poster. I had begun seeking the same sense of detachment I'd experienced during TRs in Scientology, where the object of my focus was my twin's eyes. I found that sensation again through Brahma Kumaris meditation.

One evening, though, after a longer-than-usual meditation session, I felt a growing sense of anxiety as I left the Brahma Kumaris Center. The discomfort worsened when I got behind the wheel of Dorothée's car and hit the road. I wasn't driving alertly and felt far from being in control. It dawned on me that my consciousness had been altered during the meditation.

Once at Dorothée's house, I told her about the unpleasant side effects, which I directly associated with that style of meditation. She encouraged me to continue investing in the practice to find stability. Her response didn't convince me, but I held my tongue. She had grown quite attached to this new practice, and I didn't want to jeopardize our friendship. She had already begun refusing to have sexual relations with me, and I feared she might want to end our friendship as well.

Restrictive Lifestyle

Dorothée eventually distanced herself physically from me. We still saw each other, but she refused to let me touch her. She fully embraced the Brahmin way of life, which made her increasingly inaccessible. For instance, the Brahma Kumaris advised their followers to avoid eating meat, fish, seafood, eggs, garlic, onions, and so on. As a result, it became hard for her to accept dinner invitations from non-Brahmins.

She also had to meditate every evening at four p.m. for forty-five minutes. Then, she would go to L'Émergence around seven a.m. to participate in a meditation session, followed by daily teachings, before heading to work. To keep up with this schedule, she had to be in bed by eight, which left no time for us to spend together.

> *"Almost every major cult and cult-like group we came upon teaches some form of not thinking... as part of its regular program of activity. The process may take the form of repetitive prayer, chanting or speaking in tongues, self-hypnosis, or diverse methods of meditation... Such techniques, when practiced in moderation, may yield real physical and mental health benefits. Prolonged stilling of the mind, however, may wear on the brain physically until it readjusts suddenly and sharply to its new condition of not thinking. When that happens, we have found the brain's information-processing capacities may be disrupted or enter a state of complete suspension, disorientation, detachment, hallucination, delusion, and, in extreme instances, total withdrawal."*
>
> Rick Alan Ross, CULTS INSIDE OUT.

The rules Dorothée tried to implement became more restrictive and increasingly isolated her. For my part, I could only respect her personal choices, though I couldn't help but notice she was getting entangled in yet another restrictive religious movement. The apocalyptic nature of the group she'd joined worried me deeply. What's the point of preserving the environment if we're at the end of the planet's cycle? Why bother saving for retirement or ensuring the education of young people who supposedly don't have much time left? Why care for our physical health if we only have a few years to live?

I found the idea of stopping procreation particularly harsh. It sent a shiver down my spine to imagine a world filled only with adults, no children in sight. Also. I began to worry seriously for Dorothée—especially when she mentioned considering dedicating part of an inheritance from a friend to help fund a new meditation center linked to the Brahma Kumaris.

Eventually, Dorothée told me she was going to India for a month to participate in a meditation retreat at the headquarters of the Brahma Kumaris. This did not reassure me at all. I had seen Scientologists drop everything to join the Sea Org and disappear for good. I feared this might be the last time I'd see Dorothée. However, with only my personal experiences and 'intuition' as reasons, I struggled to find a way to voice my concerns. I didn't dare tell her directly what I thought about the group, fearing she would cut the fragile bond that still held us together.

The romantic aspect of my relationship with Dorothée placed me in a tricky spot. It could've easily seemed like I was frustrated by the end of our intimate relationship, or worse, possessive or jealous. So, I simply stayed in touch, hoping she might express some doubts and want to talk. Meanwhile, I began searching for information that might support my concerns if the topic ever came up.

Looking for Information

Before discussing my apprehensions about the Brahma Kumaris with Dorothée, I wanted to ensure that my fears weren't solely fueled by my past negative experiences. So, I began seeking external opinions on the Brahma Kumaris. Just as I had done years earlier when seeking an unbiased perspective on the Mission of the Holy Spirit, I turned to the Resource and Observation Center for Religious Innovation at Laval University to consult their file on this movement.

"In 1937, Lekhraj Khubchand Kripalani initiated the Brahma Kumari movement in a village near Hyderabad, in present-day Pakistan., which would eventually grow into a global spiritual organization. At the head of a flourishing jewelry business and enjoying considerable fortune, when he was over sixty years old, Lekhraj claimed to have had a series of mystical experiences, including visions that deeply upset him." [57]

As soon as I read the first paragraphs, a question sprang to mind: Did Mr. Kripalani have these 'mystical experiences' during his time as a jeweler? I found it odd that this man proposed a form of meditation that involved contemplating a 'diamond' fixed at the center of a poster.

It seemed that the founder of the Brahma Kumaris had drawn inspiration from his profession to create a transcendental meditation technique that was similar to self-hypnosis. As I continued reading about the Brahma Kumaris, I discovered that the founder's claims extended far beyond merely developing a meditation practice.

> *"Lekhraj Kripalani claimed to have received his visions directly from the Supreme Soul, which revealed to him the true nature of man (an eternal soul borrowing a physical body)."* [58]

After reading the file from Laval University, I continued my research online. I came across several pages and sites run by organizations and centers affiliated with the new religious movement, which described the benefits of this type of meditation and promoted free courses and conferences on spirituality. I didn't dwell on these pages, as I was already familiar with this perspective shared by Dorothée and other Brahmins. They all conveyed the same message, given their affiliation with the movement.

A Cult?

Convinced I might find something to help Dorothée understand my concerns, I refined my search with terms like 'danger' and 'cult' and stumbled upon several critical websites about the movement. One in particular caught my eye. It referenced report no. 2468 from a National Assembly Commission of Inquiry in France, tabled in 1995. This report listed cultic movements active in France at that time, including the International Spiritual University of Brahma Kumaris. Given that I couldn't broach the subject with Dorothée and our relationship seemed to be deteriorating, I set aside my research, frustrated and hoping I was wrong about the new movement and that Dorothée would be all right. However, since my encounter with the Brahma Kumaris—whom I now consider dangerous—

had impacted my spiritual journey, I knew I couldn't exclude them from my book.

To validate my impressions of this religious movement, I resumed my online search before publishing. This time, I found several pages critical of the movement. The National Union of Family Defense Associations and Individual Victims of Sects (UNADFI), which I had consulted in my search for Brahma Kumaris and confirmed my initial concerns about its isolating nature.

The UNADFI, which I had consulted in my search for the Mission of the Holy Spirit was unequivocal in its condemnation of the Brahma Kumaris and confirmed my initial concerns about its isolating nature:

"Identified as apocalyptic, the movement announces the imminent destruction of the world [...] Through its practice and its supervision, detachment encourages the devotee to leave everything—assets, comfort, friends, and sentimental ties (to have a free mind to be born spiritually). Purity becomes an obsession to be part of the deity community (the rest of humanity being the demonic community). Meditation, five minutes per hour, is intended to be receptive to a spiritual message that Baba could send. Cutting off from the outside world, fatigue, obedience, and submission leads to a loss of critical thinking and a sense of responsibility." [59]

"Brahma Kumaris: a strictly millennial (End of the world) spiritualist cult sect based on the mediumistic teachings from a 'spirit entity' adherents believe is the God of all religions. 'God,' the Brahma Kumaris World Spiritual University, teaches speaks to humanity exclusively through their psychic mediums. The Brahma Kumaris World Spiritual University remains extremely secretive of its original teachings, which they call 'Sakar Murlis.' This is due to their inflammatory nature, particularly towards all other religions, which are considered to be completely 'impure' and 'degraded' [...] These 'channeled messages' are being gradually re-written by the leadership to exclude failed predictions, incorrect references, politically incorrect utterances, and lengthy repetitions, thereby

disallowing adherents and researchers alike grounds to gain a full understanding of the religion and its founder." [60]

By reading one of these 'Sakar Murlis,' which are taught to Brahmins in the early morning at various centers around the world after their period of 'special meditation,' I gained a clearer understanding of the nature of the messages from the God of the Brahma Kumaris:

"Sweet children, in order to become heirs, surrender yourselves, that is, become destroyers of attachment to everyone. Follow the Sakar Father fully."

Question: *What is the way to be saved from sin and attain blessings from many souls?*

Answer: ***To be saved from sin, surrender your body, mind, and wealth, everything—to the Father.*** *Then, look after everything as a trustee. Take Shrimat at every step. Shrimat says: You children cannot use your money for any sinful act. To donate to sinful souls is also to become an instrument in sin being committed. Therefore, **if you have wealth, open a spiritual hospital**, and you will receive blessings from many.*

It seems as if the 'Sakar Father' of the Brahma Kumaris seems rather keen on the Brahmins' money and wealth...

CHAPTER 21

A 'PERSONALIZED' SPIRITUAL JOURNEY

Although my time at the Brahma Kumaris Center was brief, the encounter had a profound impact on my spiritual journey. From the start of my practice with the transcendental meditation technique taught at L'Émergence, I noticed it offered a welcome escape from the stress in my life. So, I began meditating regularly, focusing on any point of light, unaware that I was essentially practicing self-hypnosis. A few minutes were enough for me. I wanted to avoid slipping back into a state similar to the one I had experienced, leaving the BK's center and finding myself stuck in traffic.

To quiet my thoughts, I focused on something constructive, choosing mantras of my own invention, such as 'I am calm' or 'I am great,' depending on the day's struggles. What the BKs proposed as a mantra was of little use to me. Their repetition of 'I am a spiritual being' seemed a tactic to artificially induce a state of extreme dissociation that feels like exteriorization, where one feels disconnected from their body and starts believing that their body is secondary. Since I already believed I was a spiritual entity, I didn't find it necessary.

Eventually, after a few months of practice, I no longer needed a physical point of light placed before me. I could visualize a luminous point in my mind and focus directly on it. I simply closed my eyes and saw a light in my mind, representing a 'nourishing higher power,' much like the diamond in the BK's poster symbolized the Supreme Being for them. I could now reconnect with this energy source anywhere, anytime.

France

In the spring of 2006, I had been corresponding by postal mail with a professional musician living in Toulon, France, a city nestled between Marseille and Saint-Tropez on the Mediterranean coast. She had been introduced to me by a woman I met in a park with whom I had shared my passion for opera. In her latest letter, my correspondent had included some small shells and sand in the envelope and sketched a sailboat at the bottom of the page. I took it as an invitation, interpreting it as a subtle nudge to visit her in person. Since my relationship with Dorothée was over, I decided to take the plunge and meet this French woman. I left a message on her answering machine to let her know I would be arriving in her town the following week.

Embarking on this adventure, I had no idea what awaited me. I hadn't even seen a picture of the musician, but I was determined to test my fate. Without waiting for her response, I booked a return flight to France for a week-long vacation to meet her. I planned to land in Paris and then take the high-speed train to Toulon. Excited about returning to Europe, having previously spent a few days in Germany at the International Association of Scientologists event ten years earlier, I flew out early in the morning and arrived in Paris a few hours later. I quickly made my way from Charles de Gaulle Airport to the train station, eager to catch my train. Although I was disappointed that I did not have time to explore Paris, I promised myself I would return someday.

On the train, sitting next to a French Canadian I had met, I marveled at the sight of the first palm trees and the Mediterranean Sea appearing through the windows as we approached Marseille. I gazed at the sea, lost in thought and wondering what to expect from this meeting. Once in Toulon, I wander ed around before booking a room at a budget hotel near the train station. After showering and dressing in my best clothes, I returned to the hotel reception to ask for directions to my musician friend's place. I was pleased to learn it was within walking distance. With a light heart but a touch of nerves, I strolled down the main road, admiring the historic buildings and public gardens on my left while catching glimpses of the sea on my right. I was happy to be away from Montreal, even if only for a few days.

When I arrived in front of my correspondent's building, I rang the doorbell number she had provided and waited. After about thirty seconds with no answer, I pressed the bell again, but still no response. I continued to wait and rang once more, but still, nothing. Unsure of what to do, I hesitated for a few minutes, debating whether to return to my hotel or linger in the area in case she came back. Just as I decided to head back, I had the distinct impression of seeing a curtain move on the third floor and close as soon as I looked up. I pressed the doorbell one last time, left a note with the name of my hotel under the button panel, and left, disappointed but not entirely surprised, given that I had arrived unannounced.

Back at the hotel, as I headed toward the elevator, the receptionist intercepted me and informed me that my correspondent had called. She left a message saying she had to replace another musician at short notice and would be on tour for a few weeks. Though I doubted the musician's sudden tour, it didn't matter. Without this unexpected twist, I might never have visited France, and the subsequent events would never have unfolded.

Nissa La Bella

Determined not to let this unfortunate turn of events ruin my vacation, I took a train to Nice, another coastal gem in the Côte d'Azur, about a hundred and fifty miles away. Once part of Italy, Nice still retains a strong Italian flavor. Located on the famed Côte d'Azur, it was a place I had often heard of and was eager to explore. Upon arrival, I booked a cheap room in a small hotel near the station, which turned out to be one of the seediest places I'd ever stayed. Afterward, I went in search of something to eat.

Still reeling from jet lag, I returned to the hotel early, craving a good night's sleep. But I barely slept that night. I spent the evening scratching myself due to bedbugs and squashing the little critters that scurried between m y bed and the bathroom.

The next morning, as exhausted as ever, I went to Nice's tourist office next to the train station for assistance. With a tight budget, I was steering clear of four- and even three-star hotels. I would have preferred sleeping on the beach over spending another night in that place, so I needed to find a decent and affordable alternative.

The tourist office suggested a small two-star hotel just a five-minute walk from the sea. I went straight there, inquired about the rates, and booked a room for the remaining nights of my stay in France. The next day, I headed straight to the beach to unwind. Each morning, I meditated by the vastness of the sea, closing my eyes to visualize a higher power in the form of a sun while listening to the waves and feeling the wind on my skin. It was like being in heaven. In the afternoons, I would take the bus or train to visit nearby villages, relishing the experience after the difficulties of the past years.

Noting that the hotel managers were friendly and welcoming, I offered them a can of maple syrup I had brought for my ghost musician. Later that day, one of the owners invited me to share a meal with them, which I gladly accepted. I chatted extensively during the meal, perhaps because I had been traveling alone for a few days. I recounted the recent events and how I ended up at their hotel, shared my love for music and theater, and spoke about my dream of performing in their beautiful country someday.

A couple of days later, just before my return to Montreal, I had another meal with my new friends. During that meal, they invited me to visit them during the off-season. They offered to provide a small, affordable room in the attic of their building. Delighted, I promised to return and see them again.

Back to work

Back in Montreal, I was feeling much better. I continued meditating and returned to work. At that time, I had not consumed alcohol or used drugs and had even quit smoking cigarettes for nearly three years.

Ultimately, I considered my stopover with the Brahma Kumaris a benefit since it introduced me to the habit of transcendental meditation. Gradually, I lowered my guard toward other religious movements, including those I had known since birth. After all, my practice of TRs in Scientology had prepared me for the transcendental meditation of the Brahma Kumaris. I also reminded myself that Canada's vigorous protection of religious freedom through the Canadian Charter of Rights and Freedoms should be mirrored by my own openness and tolerance toward such movements, regardless of my personal opinion of their guru or doctrine. One thing led to another, and a few months later, I let my guard down and returned to the Church of Scientology to meet a girl from the Sea Org who was related to one of my cousins. She managed to convince me to meet her in the church lobby, even though I had vowed never to set foot there again.

Upon my arrival, she immediately informed me that former members of the Sea Org could now join the staff of a lower-level organization. I firmly told her I had no intention of getting involved with Scientology again. However, it felt like talking to a wall—she ignored my words and took control of the conversation. She knew exactly which strings to pull to guide me in her chosen direction. Her spiel about humanity's survival and my previous decision to make a difference suddenly resonated with me. At that point in my life, I needed to reassess my self-esteem, and she seemed to sense that. However, my return to the staff was brief and, ultimately, turned out to be beneficial. In the days that followed, I became acutely aware of the true dangers of Scientology processing.

When the light turns on

Upon returning to the Montreal Scientology Organization staff, I was assigned the task of organizing a room filled with piles of folders containing all the information reported by the auditor by his client during auditing sessions. These had been stored in an old sauna in the building's basement—files of people who hadn't returned for sessions for some reason. There were heaps of them, many marked with a red tag, indicating that the last auditing session had gone wrong and that the person had to receive an auditing session within twenty-four hours to correct the situation. The sight of these folders stored in that locker told me a lot: these people had never returned to fix things up. Scattered among the piles were folders of individuals I had known who had suddenly vanished from the scene and never returned. Several folders were on the verge of falling apart, their contents spilling onto the floor. Eventually, I came across the file of a guy I had known since I joined Scientology at twelve. I had liked him, but now he was in a terrible state— schizophrenic and refusing help from psychiatrists.

I also realized that I had been entrusted with handling these ultra- confidential files despite having been away from the organization for several years and having openly criticized Scientology on numerous occasions. It made no sense. As I looked at the multitude of people for whom auditing had failed, a light went on in my mind. I became anxious, thinking about certain events from my own courses or sessions that might have affected me more seriously and possibly earned me a red tag as well. And I still didn't understand how they had managed to convince me to sign a new staff contract. That day, I left the organization for good. I knew I needed to stay away from anything directly or indirectly related to Scientology if I valued my mental health.

Looking the other way

In 2006, I was working downtown as a security guard for a television studio. Since I didn't have a car to commute between home and work, I had to take bus #45, which ran along Papineau Street and passed right in front of the Scientology building. I would've preferred to avoid the place altogether, but I wasn't willing to add a forty-minute detour to my trip. Every time we drove by that building, I could feel a knot of anxiety and anguish tightening in my chest and I'd look the other way. Hubbard, the guru would've had an explanation for it. After all, he was the one who'd managed to plant those beliefs in my head: I was guilty of major crimes. I was a 'degraded being' who required several hours of auditing and should be sent directly to the RPF. A thetan stuck under 2.0 on the tone scale. And I was terrified of falling again into the clutches of that organization, the same one that had so easily convinced me to sign a new staff contract against my own will, turning me into some kind of spiritual slave. What frightened me most was realizing just how far Scientologists were willing to go to manipulate me so I stay under their control. Sitting on that bus, I finally solidified my opinion of Hubbard and his dangerous cult.

Unfortunately, in the days that followed, my relationship with my father deteriorated even further, as I flatly refused to honor the contract or set foot in his church again. I was trying to maintain a connection with him, but he kept trying to pull me back into the organization. I had grown bitter about Scientology and its founder, and it showed. To make sure he understood how I felt about it, I angrily told him, *"Don't you see the trap you've dragged your wife, children, brothers, and so many friends into by bringing them into this cursed cult? You, of all people, who managed to escape The Mission!"*

Unfeeling, perched atop the Tone Scale's pinnacle, he retorted: *"You handpicked this life. You even selected me as your father, and you knew the kind of life you would have even before you came into the physical universe. Some gratitude wouldn't go amiss, considering I'm the one who gifted your corporeal form by planting my seed in your mother's garden!"*

His response made it crystal clear: I was squandering precious time arguing with this man who happened to be my father. From that day, I started doubting we could ever reconcile!

CHAPTER 22

FRANCE AS A SAFE HAVEN

As 2006 waned, I approached thirty-five, with only a few months left to apply for a visa that would grant me access to a cultural exchange program between Quebec and France. This coveted document provided young nationals from both countries with a year-long pass to the host country's job market and, to some extent, to their social services. Resolved to obtain the visa and leave midweek, I ventured to Montreal's French consulate, where I secured the visa on the spot. Swiftly, I bid Quebec adieu, aiming to nestle in southern France until spring, dodging another harsh winter. Smitten with the region from a recent visit, I couldn't resist the alluring offer from two French acquaintances. Subconsciously, I'd seized a chance to distance myself from the now-haunting Scientology and my father, whom I'd almost grown to despise.

After the Atlantic crossing, I needed several days to recalibrate. My night guard gig had taken its toll, jet lag compounding the exhaustion. The Mediterranean sun, sea, and village strolls rejuvenated me. Distance and fresh surroundings worked wonders. With ample time, I rekindled my meditation practice, gazing into the flame of a candle in my snug attic room. Still reeling from my Scientology summer nightmare in Montreal, I sought to piece myself back together, feeling like I was in mental rehab. One morning, while perusing Nice-Matin at a downtown café, a sentence caught my attention. It contained a word Hubbard had warped, assigning it a new definition within Scientology's lexicon. Initially, I tried decoding it through Hubbard's lens, realizing it didn't fit. My understanding only aligned with Scientology's twisted concept, comprehensible solely to fellow cult members. The exact word eludes me, but the isolation I felt remains vivid. That word catapulted me back to the academy, studying that barbaric nonsense. On that Nice terrace, I felt suspended between universes, momentarily transported to Montreal's academy. For a heartbeat, I relived the overwhelming helplessness from my cult-escaping days. It dawned on me: I wasn't out of the woods. I needed to unearth and discard all of Hubbard's warped concepts. Starting with that newspaper word's twisted definition, which held no meaning in the society I yearned to rejoin. My reintegration began there, with one mangled word definition.

Gradually, I started to shed the 'suppressive person' label and realized I wasn't so much a 'degraded being' either. I almost managed to absolve myself of responsibility for enduring sexual abuse and slowly started to grasp that rejecting Scientology's ethical dogma wouldn't doom me to misery.

Thirsty

France greeted me with a nagging thirst. Wine bottles beckoned from every corner of old Nice as I trekked to the sea, solitude amplifying their siren song. Knowing alcohol's destructive potential, I sought refuge in a nearby support group. Regular visits quelled my loneliness and quieted the booze-craving demons. One afternoon, midway through a meeting, that old feeling from the '93 Stanley Cup parade resurfaced, albeit muted. Again, I felt like the lone alien in the room. Discomfort silenced me as I observed others with involuntary detachment, sadness seeping in. Despite the warm welcome and genuine interest, I couldn't shake my judgmental stance and sense of being an outsider. Suddenly, the Mission of the Holy Spirit invaded my thoughts. Though long gone, its teachings clung to me: I was different, destined for a higher purpose: regeneration of humanity.

This 'specialness' had always defined me, a birthright from the cult that cost me my extended family's acceptance. Their rejection only reinforced my uniqueness. I'd embraced this belief, finding meaning in our shared tragedy - we, the consecrated children, exiled in Satan's realm.

That day, my past's grip loosened. I realized how deeply ingrained my beliefs had become, tinting my self-perception and worldview, shaping my attitudes and behaviors much like they had my father's and fellow Mission-raised individuals'. I could finally articulate years of alienation - at school, the Juvenile Center, and university. My pre-birth spiritual journey had erected an invisible barrier between me and society. This epiphany shattered the glass bubble I'd lived in for eons. Later, perched on Nice's pebbly beach, gazing at the Mediterranean, I felt a long-lost contentment wash over me. Freedom beckoned, reigniting my zest for life - reminiscent of childhood joy when Mom allowed me to play with the neighbor boy, declaring us 'out of The Mission.' I had contemplated extending my stay in Côte d'Azur indefinitely, at least until spring, as initially planned. The reality, however, had other ideas: with five euros left to my name and jobless.

Job needed

After spending several weeks in Côte d'Azur and feeling rejuvenated, I started visiting employment agencies in search of work. However, my visa seemed to confuse them, as if they wouldn't trust that I was allowed to work in France. I also handed out my CV to various places and sought assistance from the Canadian consulate, but their efforts didn't yield any results. With my return flight approaching, I had made the decision to leave in and planned to rely on credit cards until then. However, reluctant to depart, I found myself beachside, adrift in desperation. Eyes closed, I slipped into prayer, echoing that balcony moment fifteen years prior. No specific deity, just a plea for courage, strength, and a dash of hope. Then, before onlookers could spot my damp cheeks, I plunged into the Mediterranean, chasing present-moment bliss.

Back at the hotel, an email bombshell: my Montreal flight? Canceled. Options: reschedule or refund. Stunned, I sensed divine intervention telling me I should stay, so I opted for a refund on my credit card. Enthusiasm surging, I opted in. Aware of the tightrope ahead, I polished my CV, highlighting my unfinished studies in private security in Quebec. That evening, I distributed copies, a nod to the universe's whisper. Determined, I'd print an army of CVs if needed, hellbent on landing something within the week. For a first stop, I would head to the four-star Boscolo Park Hotel, the site of last week's ex-alcoholics convention I'd attended. Blocks from my digs and fifty meters from where I had prayed on the beach that same afternoon, it felt right. Even though I would only distribute one CV, it would be a way to show my willingness to the universe.

The receptionist, beaming with a smile, promised to expedite my CV to HR. My mission for that day accomplished, I retreated to my room, emotionally drained. The next morning, still sleeping at the hotel, my friend, the tenant, came knocking on my door, telling me that someone wanted to talk to me on the phone: Park Hotel HR had summoned me for an interview. I showed up, and they hired me on the spot. Incredulous at my fortune, I marveled at the contrast: yesterday, a sobbing mess on the beach; today, employed! How swiftly fate's winds can shift.

Taking a Stand

Echoing a pivot made fifteen years prior, I faced another behavioral overhaul on my inaugural night shift. Scientology, that persistent specter, materialized anew. The Citizens' Commission for Human Rights (CCHR), one of the cult's tentacle organizations opposing psychiatry, had set up shop on my new workplace's ground floor with their arsenal: photos of electroshock patients writhing in agony, Nazi camp horrors on display. Their ridiculous claim: 'Psychs' bore the blame for the Holocaust's atrocities.

My new workplace had leased a hefty chunk of its ground floor to this organization. Once again, I felt an unseen hand had guided me to this precise spot at this exact moment. Just like with my encounter with Daniel the day I came out of Denise's building, which led me to quit drugs. Another life-altering choice loomed: flee Scientology or face it head- on. No more averting my gaze like on that Montreal bus months ago! After weeks of job-hunting, I wasn't going to turn my back on a gig that would permit me to stay in France till the end of my visa. Yet here I was, staring down one of my fiercest demons. I wouldn't have to think twice. But diplomacy would be key if I wanted to keep this job!

After my first shift, I surprised myself by politely asking the reception director if renting to cults was common practice. I explained CCHR's ties to Scientology, a recognized cult in France, and shared my painful Canadian encounter with it. What mattered to me was standing tall and exposing this satellite organization without losing my cool. That morning, by calmly denouncing them, I felt another of their invisible shackles crumble. Fear of Scientology almost completely passed away; I could now face them panic-attack-free. My superior was speechless, but that was perfectly fine with me!

Luckily, my night shifts helped me dodge the daytime Scientologists manning the exhibit. Had we crossed paths, a recruitment attempt might've triggered me, probably costing me my job. Confidence rekindled during my long night shift; I scoured the internet for evidence supporting my claims to my boss. My research unveiled Scientology's murky underbelly. I discovered videos exposing the movement and its leader, David Miscavige – whose room I'd cleaned in Florida at twelve. He'd succeeded Hubbard, gaining notoriety for his inhumane treatment of staff.

I learned of recent high-profile defectors publicly denouncing Scientology. BBC and other reputable channels had aired exposés on Hubbard's pseudo-religion. One video featured a former top executive revealing how the church sneakily distributed CD-ROMs to members, installing software that blocked access to critical media websites. Accusations against Scientology organizations ran rampant: fraud, child abuse, kidnapping, forced abortions, and more. The devastating impact of their Suppressive Person policy on countless families became evident. *The Hole*, a secret prison located for Scientology executives who didn't follow Miscavige's policies, was also exposed. One filmed interview struck a chord. Five or six individuals, each having invested hundreds of thousands to scale the OT levels, shared their experiences. Shockingly, their psychological well-being deteriorated as they ascended the Bridge to Total Freedom, particularly upon reaching OT 3 and encountering the preposterous tale of *Xenu the Dictator*.

My internet deep-dive led me to an article specifically addressing OT 3, aka *The Wall of Fire*. I'd heard whispers years before. Hubbard claimed near-death while developing this level, insisting its content remain secret due to its danger to the unprepared. He even required locked briefcase transport to those deemed ready for this revelation. Apprehension gripped me as I contemplated reading it. However, firmly grounded in reality, I realized upon perusal why confidentiality was paramount. Hubbard's revelations were nothing short of hilarious, insane, and utterly incredible for someone not thoroughly prepared to swallow that kind of eccentricity.

Xenu the Dictator

In a text published without Scientology's authorization, I discovered that seventy-five million years ago, a certain Xenu, dictator of a distant galactic federation, supposedly rid his galaxy of billions of inhabitants by transporting them to Earth aboard spaceships and then exterminating them with hydrogen bombs. The unfortunate thetans emerging from these dead bodies, traumatized, were said to have since been grafted onto human bodies, spiritually parasitizing them and causing all sorts of existential problems.

OT Level 3 and most subsequent OT levels involved solo procedures where Scientologists addressed these 'body thetans' to free them from the trauma of their exile and the explosions, so they would finally leave the Scientologist 'in peace' and reincarnate elsewhere! Reading this, I realized how fortunate I was not to have endured more professional audition processes. I began to feel pity for those poor souls who had sunk deeper into the Scientology abyss.

"I have personally learned of the cases of 14 people who had full-blown mental breakdowns after completing level OT 8" Karen de la Carriere[61]

CHAPTER 23
A NEW START

While working at the Park Hotel, I met two colleagues who were getting married. I offered to sing at their religious ceremony. My performance at the Catholic Church of Saint-Laurent-du-Var marked the start of a series of magical small engagements. During my stay in France, I realized a long-forgotten musical dream that had been overshadowed by a lack of opportunity and lingering depression. I rediscovered my true self, the person I had forgotten since I was about seven or eight years old. It significantly enhanced the positive aspects of my personality and my pride in a good way.

While on the Côte d'Azur, I also had the opportunity to sing at weddings in Nice, Saint-Jean-Cap-Ferrat, and Monte Carlo. I performed at two events organized by the Canadian Club of Monaco and was eventually invited by the Monaco Red Cross to provide musical entertainment at a palliative care center in Cap d'Ail. This opportunity led to performances at several retirement homes in Nice, Beausoleil, and Monaco, where I occasionally played the guitar and sang. After performing for the Red Cross, my perspective on music underwent a drastic change. I felt more connected to people and involved in the well-being of the elderly; this greatly boosted my self-esteem and gave my life renewed meaning.

I also sang at religious services at the Anglican Church of Monte Carlo, a place I came to love and visit regularly despite not being a firm believer. There, I found a welcoming community. The priest, an American who had lived in Quebec for thirty years before relocating to Monte Carlo, became a friend. I spent a lot of time with him, sharing my vision of God, which differed from his. He accepted it and agreed to baptize me in 2008. I had wanted this since I often attended the church and felt like an impostor not being baptized.

Around that time, I also had the chance to participate in a production of Hoffmann's Tales, staged by a small opera company under the direction of Albert Lance, a tenor who had performed with Maria Callas and Joan Sutherland, and his wife, Iris Parel. Although it wasn't in a grand opera house, I felt I had realized the dream I once had when entering McGill's music faculty. Thanks to Facebook, I reconnected with a former university acquaintance in Frankfurt, Germany, who invited me to participate in a pastiche operetta he was staging in a small German theater. That summer, I spent five weeks in Germany.

Shortly after, I returned to Monaco to audition for the Monte Carlo Opera choir, which was seeking a new bass. Although I wasn't selected, it didn't matter. I knew I had made a strong impression. Simply attending the audition and performing better than ever before in front of the director, musical director, and chorus director felt like a miracle: believing in myself and seeing it through was a significant accomplishment.

Little Return to the Motherland

Two and a half years later, in March 2009, I returned to Quebec, transformed by my European adventure. Upon arriving in Montreal, I stayed at my older sister's house. She did me a massive favor by warmly welcoming me into her family. The reunion with my mother, who was present when I arrived, was touching. In 2006, when I left Quebec, I was filled with resentment and anger. However, under the Mediterranean sky, I had found forgiveness and was now in a much better mood. By realizing my dream in Europe, I reinforced my identity and became more independent and mature.

I quickly found a job in Westmount, an English-speaking borough of Montreal that was new to me. Unbeknownst to me at the time, settling there felt a bit like being abroad, and I remained the newly found person I had become in France. I also began singing in retirement homes, as I had in Europe. However, after a while, I started returning to Le Plateau-Mont-Royal, where I had spent my adolescence and part of my adult life. I had several friends there I wanted to reconnect with after all this time. Some of them frequented a café almost directly across from the Church of Scientology, so I would go there to see them.

At that time, I didn't realize it, but every time I was near the Church of Scientology, I inevitably felt awful and couldn't understand why. It was as if I was reliving the sordid memories associated with that place without seeing the images of those events. I felt ashamed and devastated inside. Scientology had cast a curse on me with its indoctrination, much like The Mission had done with my ancestors. I retained psychological scars from my time in the organization and was experiencing post-traumatic stress.

In that area, I often encountered Scientologists, as the organization was nearby. Some even came into the café to order something or just to hang out. It was unpleasant because I knew what Hubbard's followers thought of people like me who had turned away from Scientology (we were labeled Suppressive People with criminal acts we wanted to hide). One afternoon, I met the director of the organization's treasury, accompanied by their spouse. She called out to me, claiming I owed a few hundred dollars for a course I had taken after signing a new contract three years ago. That day, I surprised myself by stating I would never pay that bill and warned them not to harass me if they wanted to avoid trouble.

Around the same time, I had another intense argument with my father in that same café, which he also frequented. Unable to make him see reason, I had to tell him that if he didn't stop trying to drag me back into his damned cult, I would have to cut off contact with him. These factors contributed to my reverting to the same mindset I had in 2006, before leaving for France.

Fleeing

At the end of the summer of 2009, convinced that I would never be happy in Montreal, I returned to France with the firm intention of settling there for good. I packed all my belongings into two large suitcases and headed for Nice. There, I planned to find a place to live for a while. However, things didn't go as planned. Eventually, I even entertained the idea of living like those gypsies who sleep in cardboard boxes, though I lacked the courage for such a life. At this time, I prayed almost every night for some kind of God to take me in my sleep. Fortunately, when I was on the brink of homelessness, a friend found me a place to stay. I was tasked with overseeing a large mansion under renovation in the middle of a 'dormant' vineyard in the Var department, located between Marseille and Aix-en-Provence, approximately one hundred and fifty miles west of Nice. In this serene place, where I stayed for three to four months, I rediscovered the inner peace I had known before returning to Montreal the year before.

In solitude and near silence, I resumed meditating almost daily, either by staring at a candle or closing my eyes and imagining a powerful entity purifying me and filling me with positive energy. During my stay at the manor, I was fortunate to have access to a car. I frequently visited Marseille or Aix-en-Provence for meetings and managed to stay clean and sober. (At that time, at the end of 2009, I hadn't drunk alcohol or used drugs since September 2003). I also explored Saintes-Maries-de-la-Mer in the Camargue and the stunning town of Cassis, with its picturesque coves in the Bouches-du-Rhône. I considered myself lucky to wander through one of the world's most beautiful regions. Having distanced myself from Montreal, I felt renewed gratitude for life.

Then, winter arrived, and I began chopping wood and collecting fallen leaves from the pool and around the manor. The calm of the region forced me to confront my emotions. After a while, being so alone became challenging. However, I remained there, feeling paralyzed by the fear of the future and having nowhere else I could go. At some point, I stopped 'transcendental meditation' as it intensified my sense of solitude and started giving my anxiety. I tried to keep busy outdoors or write songs, but inspiration eluded me. Almost every day, I would drive to the nearest McDonald's for an ice cream, hoping to meet someone to chat with, but I always returned alone.

Mother is Sick

In early February, I received the devastating news that prompted my return to Montreal: I was told by my sister that Mom had stage 3 cancer and only had six months to live. The news hit me like a cold shower, especially since I had seen little of her in recent years. There was no way she could leave this world before we saw each other again and reconciled. I admitted to myself that I had been a difficult child—rebellious, cheeky, and sometimes downright wicked. I felt the need to make amends with my mother. These years in Europe had profoundly transformed me, and I wanted to show her the man I had become—still imperfect but different from the one she had known. This woman, who had endured a terrible life, deserved my presence and my support.

Upon returning to Quebec in March 2010, I immediately visited my mother. It was comforting to know I could spend time with her. Given her illness, I focused on the present rather than dwelling on the past. I aimed to make her feel that I understood many things. I knew she held no grudges, and any remorse was mine alone. I simply tried to love her and be available to her.

Still struggling to distance myself from Scientology, I returned to my favorite café in Le Plateau-Mont-Royal to reconnect with friends. But, with winter's arrival, I quickly fell back into the depression I had tried to escape by leaving for Europe. Consequently, I decided to find another refuge away from Quebec's impending winter. In the fall of 2010, another opportunity arose for me, this time in the Caribbean. I set off with my backpack on my shoulder, leaving my car parked at my brother's place in the countryside. I felt at peace with my mother, knowing she was in good hands, surrounded by my siblings. I could have stayed and waited for her to pass, but she would not have approved.

In this new country, I initially worked for someone who was referred to me. However, when I realized he had no intention of paying me, I changed my plans. I spent most of my time playing guitar and exploring the island where I had landed.

Finding Love

A few weeks after my arrival, I developed a romantic relationship with a young woman and began seeing her daily. I grew attached and envisioned starting a family with her. However, I soon found myself in a precarious financial situation and realized I would need to return to my home country, where my prospects were better. As a Canadian passport holder, I could return at any time to find a job, restore my finances, and return to the island if I wished. On the island, job opportunities for a foreigner like me, accustomed to higher standards, were nearly nonexistent.

A few days before leaving, after three months of dating, I proposed to the young woman I loved. We had spent a lot of time together, chatting and exploring the island, attending her church with her on a few Sundays. I knew we could be happy together. She accepted my proposal, making me the happiest man in the world, so we began planning our future together. Since I couldn't earn a living in her country, we agreed she would need to move with me to Canada if we were to start a family. I could no longer escape elsewhere due to depression or leave when the climate in Quebec became too dark for me to keep in a good mood. I would have to confront my demons rather than run from them. After planning our wedding for the following autumn, I returned home energized by my new plans for the future. This time, I settled far from the Plateau and its Church of Scientology because I already had a new job in that part of Montreal. It wasn't because I understood the need I had to stay away from Scientology that had traumatized me; it would take me years before I started realizing that. Being near the Church of Scientology, or even encountering Scientologists, triggered post-traumatic stress in me.

Finally, I settled in the East of Montreal, determined to maintain a positive outlook on life this time, without knowing that it was the best thing to do!

CHAPTER 24

MEETING JESUS

    In the spring of 2011, Denis, a friend I'd met at a meeting, introduced me to his church. During a conversation at the café near the Scientology organization, where I occasionally went, Denis spoke so highly of his church that I wanted to check it out. I mentioned that I was about to marry a devout Christian woman in the fall and that she would likely move with me to Quebec. I thought she might want to find a local congregation when she arrives, so when? Denis suggested I visit his church; I said, why not? I thought it couldn't hurt! After having visited the Brahma Kumaris Center with Dorothée, I found myself heading to a Pentecostal church this time.
    The building at the address Denis gave me was unlike any church I had ever known: it had no bell tower or statues. Instead, it resembled a commercial building with large windows, a spacious entrance hall with big television screens on the ceiling, and a library selling books. As I entered, I was greeted warmly by two energetic young women and a guy, which put me at ease. After we had exchanged smiles, two more friendly young women handed me a leaflet and invited me into a room. The room was nothing like the sanctuaries I was used to. It resembled a conference hall, capable of holding seven or eight hundred people, similar to those found in convention centers. That morning, there were at least five hundred people present. Intrigued, I joined Denis, who was waving from the third or fourth

row. Just as I was about to sit down next to him, musicians, followed by a singer and choir, took the stage.

I really liked the type of music they played. The lively atmosphere felt more like a concert with high-quality sound than a mass. I was immediately charmed by the rhythms and the soft-rock-style melodies. Like most of the crowd, I stood and sang the hymns, following the lyrics scrolling on giant screens on either side of the stage. After a few minutes, I poured my heart into it, losing myself in the experience. It felt great to be surrounded by people, as I had spent far too much time alone since returning from the Caribbean. The musicians eventually gave way to a speaker who announced it was time for tithes and offerings. He encouraged everyone to joyfully donate 10% of their weekly income, with an additional offering for those who wished. Although I wasn't about to drop $50–60 in the bag, I was so delighted with the free concert that I pulled out a bill from my wallet. As the collection bags were passed around and the music played softly, I noticed several people raising envelopes to heaven and praying over their donations. Proudly, I placed my money in an envelope too, held it up, and let it fall into one of the circulating bags.

The service continued with announcements on the giant screens: upcoming congresses, outdoor weeks for the youth group, singles meetings, cell leader training, and more. It was fascinating. I could see that there was a vibrant community in this church. The cells, consisting of twelve members around a leader, met weekly to pray, study the Bible, and connect with one another. This concept appealed to me, given my loneliness after spending four years abroad and being away from Le Plateau — plus the fact that I was in love with a woman who lived in another country.

A Savior

After a few minutes, the announcements ended, and the music resumed. The entire room began to sing again, cheering for the man who took the stage: their pastor, Alfred, whom I had heard of before on television. He entered amid the assembly's cheers: it was clear from his confident demeanor that this charismatic man was skilled with crowds. I listened intently, captivated by his sermon. He spoke as if he were addressing me personally, talking about a savior who could lift the burdens of those who had faced difficult lives, those who had 'missed the mark,' as he phrased it. His message resonated deeply with me. Despite having stopped using drugs and alcohol for around ten years, living in sunny countries, studying music at a university, singing for both the wealthy and less fortunate, and being engaged to a wonderful woman, I still struggled with a persistent gray cloud that seemed to have taken domicile in my chest. I had yet to find lasting inner peace, and I felt as though I was rotting inside. In a few months, I would marry a young woman who seemed like a saint compared to me, and I was terrified. Since I had committed to this girl who regularly attended Christian gatherings, I had wrestled with these questions: Would she stay by my side if she knew the truth about me? Should I lie to her forever? Having known decay and darkness, having drowned myself in drugs and alcohol, would she still want to start a family with me if she knew the depth of my internal struggle?

    I could hear Pastor Alfred shifting topics, pulling out his Bible to dissect one of the many verses, but I was no longer listening. I was absorbed in my own self-reflection and guilt. At the end of the service, when the pastor invited anyone who wished to accept Jesus as their Savior to join him at the front, I didn't hesitate for long. At first, out of pride, I couldn't bring myself to get up from my seat. But seeing a few others move forward, I gathered the courage to rise and join them in front. I had been waiting for that kind of miracle for too long. I felt I had nothing to lose. Pastor Alfred greeted us with a tone of compassion and empathy, a stark contrast to the coldness I had experienced in Scientology. It touched a part of me that was crying out for comfort. He instructed us to close our eyes, and I resolved to engage fully, hoping it might ease the pain that had resurfaced. The pastor said, *"Imagine Jesus standing before you."* He continued, *"Touch him! Feel his linen garment between your fingers."* I followed his instructions, finding it easy to visualize Christ standing before me, replacing the luminous point I had been used to visualizing during my transcendental meditation. Almost instantly, just as I had seen that comforting light representing my higher power, I now saw Jesus vividly in my mind. I looked him directly in the eyes, hoping to draw his attention and reassure myself of his presence. His fair-complexioned face, with soft features and blue eyes framed by long wavy brown hair cascading over his shoulders, matched the image from Zeffirelli's film that had been etched in my mind.

Lost in contemplation, I forgot the hundreds of people behind me and put my heart into it. At that moment, after a few seconds of awe, I saw Jesus lean toward me and place his hand on my forehead. The Son of God himself had come to lay his hand on me to consecrate me. At that moment, I felt a profound sense of love and acceptance like never before and broke down in tears. Pastor Alfred then asked us to recite a prayer with him, which I did, fully committed, still with tears in my eyes. I prayed with all my heart, asking Jesus to free me from the shame and suffering I carried within. Intensely moved by this intense moment, I turned around and realized everyone in the room was watching us. Only then did I regain my senses, feeling embarrassed by the scene.

Ashamed of the tears on my cheeks, I wanted to leave. However, the pastor asked us to accompany one of his assistants to another room, where she had a small welcome gift for us. I hesitated, feeling the need to step back and process what had just happened. Yet, encouraged by the friend who invited me and by Pastor Alfred, I decided to follow the assistant. In that room, a kind lady briefly spoke to us before community members approached, offering a gift bag with a mug bearing the church's name and a small book. They then asked for our address and phone number. Having encountered similar recruitment tactics in Scientology, I was hesitant to share my contact details. However, I eventually relented, providing only my phone number before leaving with a lighter heart.

In the days that followed, I found myself smiling whenever I thought about my experience at the church. The interaction with Jesus that day had been so comforting that I felt deeply transformed. However, despite this, I had no intention of joining the Christian community. My visit had been primarily to see if it would be a suitable place for my future wife, should she wish to attend. That is what I repeated to Patrick, a church member who contacted me a week or two later, inviting me to return for another Sunday service.

During my phone conversations with Patrick, I shared my experience from that Sunday morning. I told him how deeply moved and transformed I felt by my 'encounter' with Jesus and how good I had felt, one of the rare times in my life. But I also mentioned that I didn't need to return to his church—Jesus had already done his work with me, and that was enough! I knew my idea of a loving God was unconventional and personal, but it worked for me. I didn't want to challenge my vision by discussing it with anyone. Besides, my 'inner voice' was trying desperately to tell me that I had already explored enough religious movements. But instead of listening, I let Patrick persuade me. The members of the community had been welcoming and friendly during my first visit, and Pastor Alfred's passion and charisma made his sermons bearable. And since I was also seeking to alleviate my loneliness, I found Patrick to be a pleasant acquaintance and was easily persuaded.

The next Sunday, once again, I was captivated by the festive atmosphere, largely due to the music and gospel singing, which I thoroughly enjoyed. Before long, I eagerly attended the Sunday morning assemblies at this independent Pentecostal church, mostly to sing and worship. I loved the thirty minutes of Christian music that kicked off the Sunday meeting. I immersed myself in it, singing with all my heart. I celebrated in the back of the hall, watching the faithful gathering at the foot of the stage, dancing in before the amused pastor. I was enchanted by the energy in the room when parishioners stood up and began to jump on the spot or spin like whirling dervishes, entering states of trance and mystical ecstasy.

The hymns encouraged us to get physically involved as we sang along with the congregation. I recall one African anthem we sang regularly, as the pastor, like a square dance caller, directed us to turn or 'change direction' according to the verses, which I loosely translated as: 'I am in immense joy because Yahweh has set me free.' It was particularly exhilarating!

Another song had us chanting Jesus' name, hands in the air: *"Jesus! Jesus! Jesus! Jesus! Jesus!"* It was as mesmerizing as a political rally. There was something euphoric about singing with body and soul, united with five to six hundred people, hands raised to the Lord. It was as powerful as the Brahma Kumaris' transcendental meditation. Quickly, I became fond of praising my higher power. Through this activity, I felt I could connect directly with God through the Holy Spirit in the room. I was at the pinnacle of my spiritual journey, praising my God like the Na'vi do in the movie Avatar, under the Tree of Souls, recharging my batteries connected with Eywa. I closed my eyes and saw that healing light before me—it had happened naturally since I had developed the habit of focusing on a point of light with the Brahma Kumaris. Now, I was literally entering into communion with this source of happiness, singing with arms raised to embrace it. I became addicted to it, and it would take me further than I had ever imagined.

CHAPTER 25

ENLIGHTENMENT

One Sunday morning, during an intense moment of praise at church, I found myself singing a song by Michael W. Smith: *"Let it rain, let it rain, let it rain. Open the floodgates of Heaven."* I saw the Holy Spirit descend upon me like a sparkling shower, thousands of tiny raindrops shimmering in the air before me. In that moment, I experienced true ecstasy, feeling myself cleansed of all sin. Filled with gratitude, I felt blessed—chosen, like Paul on the road to Damascus, bathed in heavenly light. My love for Jesus grew even stronger that day. However, the suffering and my feeling of shame lingered, even though I believed in God's love for me. So, I kept my spiritual practices, which only grew more intense.

A few weeks later, while reading the Bible early one morning—after meditating 'Brahma Kumaris style,' sitting before a candle, and singing praises with my guitar—I became utterly convinced that the Holy Ghost had baptized me, reaching a peak in my spiritual journey. That morning, a verse seemed to lift off the page, float in the air before me, and then drift straight into my mind through my third eye. I was stunned all over again. The entire day, I felt like I was floating on a pink cloud, which was exactly what I needed to escape my dull, gray daily life!

Now, considering myself a true apostle, baptized in the Spirit, I wanted to get involved in welcoming newcomers and helping them—just as Patrick had done for me. So, I signed up for the Leader Course, a preliminary training program for individuals who wish to guide other Christians within the church.

The course, divided into three levels, was taught by Level Three leaders and associate pastors in another building belonging to Pastor Alfred's church, located just across the street. Eager to learn how to become a better leader, I dove right in. I had fully intended to invest in this apprenticeship, something to occupy me while I waited for my wife's visa; yet, from the very first day, I realized this course had little to do with actual leadership. It was mainly about teaching us Pastor Alfred's vision of Christianity, which turned out to be quite different from mine.

I'd my own understanding of the faith, shaped by my time spent in Catholic churches, where I'd sung years ago, and by the Anglican church I'd attended a few years earlier in Monaco, not to mention the experiences I've had in recent weeks at this church. The concept of God I now held suited me perfectly, and I certainly didn't need someone to tell me how it worked, so I quickly dropped out of the course. Still wanting to stay involved in the movement, I began searching for a ministry to join. I even got baptized again—this time with full immersion by Pastor Gilbert, Patrick's leader, in the municipal pool near the church, hoping for another moment of ecstasy, which, unfortunately, never came. However, an incident pushed me to rethink my involvement and become more critical of the religious movement and its leaders.

Gurus

In early autumn 2011, on a Saturday afternoon, Patrick—who had officially become my leader—and I arrived a bit late for a meeting. The event, organized by Pastor Gilbert, the same man who had baptized me a week prior, was intended to be casual — a chance to socialize and get to know other men from the church. However, as we entered the room, I saw a group of men standing with their hands raised to heaven, praying to the '*LORD of Hosts*'— a term for God that clashed with my image of a loving deity. At the front stood Pastor Gilbert, that man who had baptized me a few weeks before. He was in a trance state, speaking in tongues: "Auh raba chumki baba chumko...," apparently channeling God. It was impressive, to say the least.

As Patrick and I approached to sit down, Gilbert snapped out of his trance and exclaimed, "I feel a lot of shame and sadness in the room." After a few moments, he walked toward me, raised his hands, and tried to place them on my head, all while speaking in tongues again. Feeling targeted by his earlier comment, I stepped back to avoid his touch. There was no way I was going to let this man gain any authority over me.

Seeing my refusal to submit, Gilbert stepped back and said, in an almost arrogant tone, "You will see miracles in this church, and you will be transformed." I wanted to reply, to tell him I'd already seen plenty of miracles in my life—that, in fact, I was a miracle myself. Not wanting to cause a scene or unsettle his devoted followers, I kept quiet. After the meeting, though, I approached Pastor Gilbert and told him that his approach had been inappropriate and clumsy, bordering on contemptuous. I added that the way he spoke to me made me feel like he saw me as inferior. From that day on, a quiet conflict began to brew between us.

Since I enjoyed the atmosphere in the church and wanted to stay connected, I asked if I could be assigned to another one of Pastor Alfred's associates within the church's pyramid structure. However, I was told that this community valued reconciliation and that I should seek to make peace with my current leaders. They expected me to remain in my original position within the church's hierarchy. Dissatisfied, I decided to attend Sunday services only, focusing on the fantastic praise and worship that never failed to feed my soul with the Holy Spirit.

Pastor Alfred

As the days went by and I struggled to integrate into the community, I gradually found myself drifting away, feeling out of place due to my growing differences. Despite floating on a pink cloud from the recent enlightenment I'd experienced, I wasn't completely blind. I couldn't ignore what I was seeing in the church. Week after week, I witnessed more or less the same catchy sermons and orchestrated performances, all designed to give seekers like me an intoxicating taste of 'salvation.' It wasn't necessarily a bad thing, provided it was done out of love and selflessness. However, I began to question the charismatic pastor's intentions.

I started to resent Pastor Alfred's attitude toward his disciples, who practically worshipped him. For instance, one Sunday morning, he chastised those who hadn't attended a conference the church had held the day before. He seemed to take pleasure in reprimanding anyone who didn't follow his instructions to the letter. In my eyes, he began to resemble more of a narcissist than a spiritual leader—more a dictator than a guide. On another Sunday, he invited a guest pastor to speak against a group of former disciples with whom he had a falling out. The guest went so far as to liken them to 'bucks with horns,' publicly excluding them from the flock of good lambs in the room, essentially branding them as beasts.

I saw in Pastor Alfred the same trait I had noticed in Hubbard—a refusal to tolerate any dissenting opinions. Like Eugène Richer La Flèche and Gustave Robitaille, Pastor Alfred didn't hesitate to interpret the Holy Scriptures to his advantage. One evening in December, he loudly proclaimed that, like him, Jesus wore only the finest clothes made of the best linens. It was his way of justifying the luxurious attire he and his wife flaunted. That evening, she wore a white sable fur coat. I didn't object to how they dressed, but I couldn't stand the way he twisted scripture to suit his narrative.

Money, money!

A few weeks before Christmas, the church played a video of Pastor Alfred wishing everyone a happy holiday season during the Sunday service. In the video, he remarked that he was "well aware that Christmas had become too commercial," then added, with questionable humor, that "despite that, he still accepted gifts." I found his humor particularly insidious and far from spiritual. On another Sunday, the congregation was asked to contribute to a collection for a birthday gift for the pastor's wife—as if they were in need! These people were already wealthy, yet Pastor Alfred seemed willing to do anything to enrich himself and his family further. It was absurd. I even began to think that after forty years in the ministry, he had become jaded, now simply entertaining himself by seeing how far he could push the envelope.

I was outraged by the constant financial demands. Aside from the regular Sunday collections, we were also asked for more money during the smaller meetings held in leaders' homes, not to mention the countless paid events—conferences, congresses, concerts—where 'real Christians' were expected to attend or risk public shaming during Sunday services. I was also shocked when I learned that they sold recordings of Sunday sermons for $10. The more I got to know Pastor Alfred, the more I suspected that a significant portion of the profits went directly into his pocket, given that he owned the copyright to his speeches and the books he sold in the church lobby. There were also healing events, where Pastor Alfred claimed to cure cancer and restore hearing to the deaf. I didn't believe any of it. To me, it was just another tactic to draw people in so they could pass the collection bag around. Eventually, I grew tired of the pressure Patrick and others put on me to conform—pay my tithe, join a department, and volunteer. It became clear that the church's primary focus was recruiting new members to feed its pyramid structure.

When I shared my observations with Patrick, he immediately began distancing himself from me. I realized then that there were two types of Christians in their eyes, and I was on the wrong side. Things got really bad between Patrick and me when I suggested that if Pastor Gilbert could speak in tongues, I could be touched by the Holy Ghost in the same way. Patrick laughed at me. His reaction spoke volumes about what he thought of me. Having been involved in religious movements before, I knew it would be impossible to effect any change. The best I could do was express my discontent to avoid feeling guilty for turning a blind eye, yet again, to despicable behavior from religious leaders.

Grief

At that time, in 2013, my mother was still alive despite the grim prognosis given three years earlier. She even accompanied me to the airport to welcome my wife, who had finally received her visa and was coming to settle with me in Quebec. In the weeks leading up to that, I had also received my high school diploma, which I'd completed through distance learning. It felt like a promising start to the year. But things quickly took a harsh turn. In the spring, my older brother passed away from a heart attack, and a few months later, in September, my mother followed him. After losing them, I grew closer to my father. On Sunday afternoons, I often met with him at a café near the Scientology organization. Our conversations had become more bearable since he seemed to have finally understood that I wasn't returning to Scientology. One afternoon, he confessed, *"When you were four or five years old, you cried constantly, and I couldn't stand it."*

I wasn't surprised to hear that. That period of my life aligned with The Warning in The Mission. Mom was stressed and didn't have time to care for me, and I was desperate for attention, especially from him. I had turned five in 1976, the same year we left The Mission of the Holy Spirit. That drastic change had been difficult for him as well. I'd heard him say more than once how painful it had been to find himself with eight children after leaving the cult he was born into at the age of twenty-nine.

Even now, decades later, I still long for his attention and love. That day, I remembered my mother once saying, *"Your father didn't want that life. He enjoyed touring with the cycling team and selling programs."* At the time, I didn't understand what she meant, but that phrase stayed with me until it finally made sense.

It took me a while to understand that my father was never meant to have a big family, as people in The Mission did. Having eight children was way too much for him and ruined his life. His free will regarding the foundation of a family had been stolen from him by the cult he was born in. During another one of our meetings, he told me: *"After leaving The Mission of the Holy Spirit, I often thought about suicide."* I wasn't surprised by this, either. I had already heard him talking about it. And all that mattered was that he didn't do it. That was the state of mind my father was in when he first stepped into the Church of Scientology.

In that dangerous, cult-like New Religious Movement, he found attention and hope for a better future —a utopian vision of changing humanity that seemed to make sense to the dream he'd chased when starting his family in The Mission. He was so enthusiastic about it that he brought many others into it with him. Later, in 2014, at the same café, Dad confided in me again, as he had a few times before: "*I don't want to live to be old. I could leave this world today. I've had enough.*"

The first time I'd heard him say that, years earlier, I hadn't taken it seriously, though it was sad to hear. But now, with my mother and older brother gone, his words took on a much heavier meaning. Moved, I responded, "*Why do you say that? Don't you realize some people care about you? You have children and grandchildren who love you and might want you to live a long life.*"

It was my way of telling him that I loved him. Dad blushed but remained silent, clearly embarrassed by our father-son moment. It wasn't his way—he had never even hugged me once in my life. But I knew I had touched his heart. A few months later, Dad died of a heart attack at the age of sixty-six.

CHAPTER 26

A NEW CHURCH

At the end of 2014, my wife and I began attending a new Christian assembly occasionally. Shortly after she arrived in Quebec, my sweet darling visited Pastor Alfred's church a few times. However, she disapproved of its pyramidal structure, where people seemed to monitor each other's behavior. That solidified my decision to avoid that church. Yet, after a while, I started to miss the 'blissful' feeling I experienced during the periods of praise. I also felt that my new status as an 'apostle of Jesus,' enlightened by the few events I had experienced at Pastor Alfred's church, only made sense if I glorified Him within a Christian community. My wife, raised in a Christian family, also wanted to find a place where she could live her faith and pray. These factors eventually led us to a small assembly near our home. It was a tight-knit community of around sixty people, who, apart from the Bible and the hymns sung during praise, had nothing in common with Pastor Alfred's church.

During one of the first assemblies in that church, the senior pastor—who seemed stern and had held the position for many years—announced his resignation. I then had the opportunity to witness the arrival of a new pastor, a man in his late fifties named Gaston, who was stepping into this role for the first time in his life. In the first year, we attended church regularly without getting involved. Personally, I had learned my lesson and preferred to keep my distance. All I wanted was to give glory to Jesus and connect with the Holy Spirit through singing praises. Of course, I could have done this at home, but the impact wasn't the same as when I joined others in singing and praying. Still, I was cautious about getting too close to the community, hoping to avoid any new conflicts after my bad experiences at Pastor Alfred's church. However, due to the small size of the church hall, it was hard to avoid people entirely. Over time, I developed a sense of belonging to this community and got familiar with some of its members, including Pastor Gaston, whom I would eventually visit in his office whenever I felt alone or worried about my future, hoping to find someone to talk to.

During my first meeting with the pastor in the office in the spring of 2016, I discovered a completely different person from the one who preached on Sunday mornings. Perhaps because he lacked Pastor Alfred's charisma, qualities, and experience, pastor Gaston played a role when he preached. He wasn't authentic, and it was clear to me. He dressed differently for Sunday service, often wearing a black suit and a black shirt with a red tie that made him look like a mafioso. He also spoke with a different tone, as if he wanted to impress and take ascendancy over the congregation present in the hall.

I much preferred the man I met in his office that day over the one who sometimes delivered fiery rants about 'the state of the world' or the presence of voodooism in the community. Still, I avoided bringing it up with him, knowing it was a delicate subject.

Men of God

From that point on, I visited my new friend, whom I began calling by his first name, every week. He lent me Christian books, which I eagerly read, and I'd ask him to clarify certain passages. I also posed questions about specific Bible verses to see if I was grasping their meaning correctly, according to him. Over time, he began calling me a 'Man of God,' a title reserved for devout Christians. Little by little, I came to see him as a mentor, trusted his guidance, and considered him as a friend. One afternoon, I even attempted to open up about my past—the cults I'd grown up in, the sexual aggressions, my time in the Juvenile Center, drug addiction, and alcoholism... I shared that I had recently lost both my parents and my older brother. But Gaston didn't seem to care either to listen. What mattered to him was what I could do for his church.

I then began listening to him. He spoke about his ambitions—his dream of a large, prosperous church, similar to Pastor Alfred's, complete with a spacious building, ample parking, and a state-of-the-art sound system. Realizing that Gaston wasn't ready to engage with the topics I needed to discuss, I asked him to recommend a Christian therapist. He introduced me to a friend of his, a psychology graduate who offered an intensive, three-day program. For three consecutive afternoons, I met with this man and discussed everything I've shared in this book—and more. I cried a lot, made resolutions for the future, and went home feeling like I had finally made peace with my past. Naturally, I shared my experience with Gaston since the therapist was his friend. I told him how much I had cried, but Gaston didn't seem to care; what he wanted was for me to serve.

In the following weeks, Gaston mentioned his plans to establish a department within the church that would assist individuals with personal struggles. I agreed wholeheartedly—the need for this type of service was obvious to me. I had already noticed that Gaston struggled to address certain topics that would surely arise when people sought guidance from that department. He suggested I train as a pastoral counselor, and I jumped at the opportunity. After all, I had dreamed of holding that position at Pastor Alfred's church, and since childhood, I had wanted to help people and make a difference in the world. I had even joined the Sea Org in pursuit of that goal. On Gaston's recommendation, I quickly enrolled in a well-known theological institute to pursue a Certificate in Pastoral Counseling. I was thrilled at the prospect of eventually helping people in distress, as I had been helped so many times before.

From that day forward, Gaston invited me to participate in the church's leadership and men's committees. It was there that I became better acquainted with Mr. Grelot, a man who glared at me every time I spoke and reminded me of some unpleasant people I'd dealt with in the past. Unfortunately for him, I no longer tolerated such attitudes toward me and took my place, pushing through with my ideas, as I did for the car wash fundraiser a few weeks later in the fall.

Gaston and Satan

Naturally, as with every movement I'd been involved in before, there were a few things about this new church that rubbed me the wrong way. One of them was Gaston's obsession with Satan. I thought about asking him to tone it down, but it was a delicate subject, so I never did. Over the past two years, I'd heard Satan's name mentioned more times than I could count during Sunday assemblies. Sometimes, it was even theatrically staged. A few months earlier, for instance, Gaston had invited an actor to perform a monologue on hell, complete with illustrations of what eternity in hell might look like for those who didn't believe in Jesus.

On another occasion, Gaston brought in a pastor who specialized in Satan. That man spent forty-five minutes discussing the devil and then promised to return later that year for a special conference titled "How Satan Acts in the World." The thought of having to sit through that again gave me chills. I found it disturbing, and there was nothing positive in Gaston's constant return to this topic. Still, I didn't bring it up with him. Without realizing it, though, hearing about hell so often during these assemblies began to seep into my mind. I started to wonder if it might actually be real.

One morning, as Satan was once again the focus of the sermon, I found myself questioning what had happened to my older brother, my mother, and my father after their deaths—since they hadn't believed in Jesus. Of course, I quickly rejected the idea that they could be burning in hell, but the constant talk of Satan had planted seeds of doubt in my head that I couldn't easily shake.

September 2016

A few weeks later, Pastor Gaston mentioned Satan several times during his sermon, looking directly at me as I sat in the second row. That's when I abruptly fell from the pink cloud I had managed to float on for the past few years. That morning, while he ranted about the fall of Satan—a character I hadn't even believed in before joining this church—Gaston shattered the illusion that Jesus had chosen me to be His apostle at Pastor Alfred's church. In the span of a single sermon, he turned me back into a son of Satan. He destroyed me, putting me in little pieces—I had faced many difficult trials in my life, but I had never felt so utterly deprived as I did that morning. Later on, that day, after dinner, I devoured an enormous piece of sugar pie, hoping it would help me forget the horrible day I'd had. But what I was about to go through was anything but 'a piece of cake.'

Finally, I never returned to Pastor Gaston's church, realizing that this man was a danger to people like me. Fortunately, I was married to a woman who had faced many challenges herself and stood by my side even as my world crumbled. It was then that I began a serious self-reflection, starting with why I kept bouncing from one religious movement to another—sometimes landing in dangerous cults or under the influence of narcissistic predators. Part of the answer came to me during one of the sleepless nights that followed the event. I had a flashback from my childhood—I could see myself standing in the entrance hall of the Scientology organization in Montreal, reading the Creed of the Church of Scientology:

"The study of the mind and the healing of illnesses of mental origin should not be separated from religion, nor tolerated in non-religious areas."

In these pseudo-religions, I sought solutions to my psychological distress, which stemmed mainly from the sexual abuse and parental abandonment I endured in my childhood. For a time, it seemed to work, thanks to various processes that helped me disconnect from my reality. But soon, a different kind of search began for me—one that would take much longer than the so-called miraculous cures I had once experienced. It all started in the weeks that followed while I was alone at home. That day, I had another severe anguish attack. Desperate, I closed my eyes and asked, *"What is wrong with me?"* Exhaustion had overtaken me, as I hadn't slept much in the past week. I hadn't touched alcohol in thirteen years, but for the first time in ages, I thought about finding a bridge, grabbing a couple of bottles of scotch, and drinking myself to death. As I sat alone on my sofa, a memory suddenly surfaced: I saw myself, about twenty years earlier, living at my father's place while trying to finish my music degree. I was behind on rent by a month or two, explaining to him that I was waiting for a deposit to come through the following week. He stood there, yelling that I was wasting my time with music. I saw him pointing his finger at me, shouting, "*You're a loser! A loooser... That's what you are!*" I remembered how I almost hit him in my rage. At that moment, sitting on the sofa, my anxieties eased a little. I had finally reconnected with a suffering I had avoided for too long. The voice in my chest had found another breach to express itself.

A few days later, sitting in my room, meditating in front of a candle, I received another '*call from my inner voice.*' This time, I didn't ignore it. It said, "*Stop searching for transcendence. Look inside your heart. Reconnect with yourself, recognize yourself, love yourself...*"

Without hesitation, I got up and sat at the foot of my bed. In a meditative state, I gazed at myself in the mirror on the wardrobe door and began repeating: "I am good. I deserve the best. I love myself..." I then remembered that 'low tone' song I had written and thrown in the garbage when returning to Scientology twenty-five years ago:

You, the neighborhood child, next-door neighbor, I saw you cry.
You who left school, overcome by the mad desire to follow an idol.
Listen to your heart, and talk to me about it,
Don't be ashamed and tell me, because in you somewhere is hidden a part of my past.

I stood in front of the mirror for a few minutes, staring into my eyes as if I were doing TRs with another student. I entered more deeply into the trance state I was already in, triggered by my focus on the candle, as I sought to break through the wall I'd built over the years. I focused intensely, wanting to connect with that part of myself that had been tugging at me for ages. Convinced I had made contact with my inner self, I repeated the words like a mantra: I love you… I love you… I love you… emphasizing certain syllables, hoping they finally land. Then, in the dim light of my bedroom, I saw my face transform into my father's. Each of my features became his as if he had come back for me. The words coming out of my mouth became his, and he finally told me the words I had always wanted to hear from him: "I love you."

EPILOGUE

"It is not by looking at the light that we become luminous, but by plunging into its darkness. But this work is often unpleasant, therefore unpopular."
Carl Gustav Jung

    I began writing this book in the summer of 2016 without fully understanding what I was after. At that time, I had an intense thirst for authenticity. Up until then, I'd only written fictional works, or so I thought, since the songs, poems, stories, and novels I'd written always reflected my own experiences. Something I wouldn't realize until after the work was finished. Once I understood this, I started writing pieces that were still inspired but firmly grounded in reality. I allowed myself to 'descend' into the low tones I had avoided since my return to Scientology in my early twenties. Authenticity became a recurring theme in my first 'realistic' writings. My shadow side had been hidden for too long. I needed to reconnect with it to find my wholeness and stop running from reality by seeking altered states of consciousness.

    I couldn't just hide alone in my bedroom, staring into the mirror, fantasizing that I could change how I saw myself and the world around me. That would only make things worse. It was time to admit that I had suffered deeply, that I had been a victim, and that I wasn't capable of bearing the weight of the world's sins as Jesus had. I needed to face the suffering I had carried since childhood. Sort out my part of the responsibility and give the rest to its owners.

In the fall of 2016, after seeing my father appear in the mirror— despite him having died two years earlier—I stopped all transcendental practices aimed at alleviating my pain because I became afraid for my mental health. I started to see the real dangers that being in cults had confronted me with. I then started deprogramming, rejecting the maximum I could of the false beliefs they had indoctrinated me with. Something more easily said than done, particularly for those that came from Scientology.

Then came the 'MeToo' movement in 2017. Seeing all those people reclaiming their lives made me understand that I, too, had to face my abusers. In the following weeks, I reported Sylvio's father to the Montreal Police Department. However, after all these years, they couldn't find him. I also reported Arthur to the Quebec City Police, only to be told that, despite ongoing legal proceedings against him in a child pornography case, they couldn't uphold my complaint because the incidents occurred in another country°! After seeing these attempts fail, I gave up trying to track down the criminal lawyer who had filmed me with my father's girlfriend more than thirty years before.

I also wanted to denounce the sectarian excesses I had experienced in the cults I had been part of, but I couldn't find any authorities to make my complaints. Seeing the need for such a department, knowing that many countries had one, I joined a group of ex-members of cults and collateral victims. Together, we submitted a petition to Quebec's National Assembly in 2018, requesting a national inquiry into sectarian excesses happening freely in 'New Religious Movements' active in our province. However, it was "pushed under the carpet" by Minister Kathleen Weil, who instead asked sociologist Loraine Derocher to address the situation.

Later that same year, I attended a training course proposed by that sociologist. A course designed for stakeholders, including psychologists, social workers, and police officers, on the topic of religious sects and closed communities. At the end of the 2-day training class, I left feeling strongly disappointed and choked, mostly because I thought, based on my experience, that the information provided in the course was either inaccurate or misleading.

This is when I decided to complete this book. If I weren't allowed to speak to the leaders of Québec's society, at least I would still be heard by some of you.

However, at that time, I realized I was still too fragile to be confronted with people who would try to silence me. To regain my mental focus, I sought help from a professional. A scientific one who had no ties to any psycho-spiritual practice, who would listen to what I had to say without leading me into another spiritual trap. I had stopped using drugs and alcohol many years earlier, and couldn't escape by leaving in other countries. It was now time to stop escaping into transcendence, which had become another form of dependency.

Now, as I finish this book, I have finally climbed out of the nauseating well I fell into as a child— mainly by learning to swim in it. No matter how painful my past has been, I have reclaimed it by confronting it, primarily through this book. As for my spiritual beliefs, I am convinced there is a force in the universe that has guided me more than once and that will always be there for me. Today, I have a great life and much more abundance than I deserve. Life is good with me, more than I can put into words, and far beyond my understanding.

NOTES

1 2 3 4 5 6 7 8 9, Freely translated by the author.
10, ALTERNATIVE SPIRITUALITY AND RELIGION REVIEW 7:2 (2016), Quebec's Holy Spirit Incarnate: The Transformation of a Marian Prayer Group into la Mission de l' Esprit-Saint.
11, Madam Palmer regularly collaborates with CESNUR, an Italian organization that defends new religious movements. She also contributed to the writing of a book unduly biased in Scientology's favor and one outrageously objective on the Raeliens, in which she forgot to mention the multiple complaints regarding that New Religious Movement.
12, Gloire à la très sainte Trinité, par Notre-Dame du Sacre -Coeur de la Régénération.
13, Freely translated by the author.
14, www.mind.org.uk/information-support/types-of-mental-health-problems/dissociation-and-dissociative-disorders/about-dissociation/
15, Poor Man's Psychoanalysis? Newsweek, November 6, 1950
16, New York Times, September 1950
17, Winter, A Doctor's Report on Dianetics
18, 27 November 1963, Report of the Honorable Kevin Victor Anderson, Victoria, Australia
19, John A. Lee, 1970, Sectarian Healers and Hypnotherapy Scientology"
20, Foster, John, December 1971 "Enquiry into the Practice and Effects of Scientology"
21, Operating Thetan is a spiritual entity that has control over matter, energy, space, and time. Literally, an 'operating spiritual being.'
22, Atack, Jon. Let's sell these people A Piece of Blue Sky. Richard Woods.
23, 27 November 1963, Report of the Honorable Kevin Victor Anderson for the State of Victoria, Australia
24, Prince, Jesse. The Expert Witness: My Life at the Top of Scientology. Prince Publishing
25-26-27, See free online Scientology course on how to raise children 07-2017
28, Mission de L'Esprit-Saint, Publication interne, Les Propos 6, page 98
29, British journalist, author of fifteen books who won multiple press awards.
30, Miller, Russell, 1987, Bare-Faced Messiah
31, Children, Scientology Handbook Series, Original Version 214
32, www.gs-formation.com/quest-ce-que-linduction-hypnotique-Freely translated.
33, www.webmd.com/mental-health/dissociation
34, Therapist and former born-in Jehovah's Witness, author of Cracking the Cult Code for Therapists
35, Hippolyte Bernheim was born on April 17, 1840, in Mulhouse and passed away on February 2, 1919, in Paris. He graduated in medicine and neurology in

1867 from the University of Strasbourg and became a lecturer at the same university the same year. In 1879, he was appointed a full professor of medicine at the University of Nancy, where he gained fame for his profound understanding of hypnosis. Sigmund Freud was significantly influenced by Bernheim. He translated one of his books and visited him in 1889.

36, A 'Clear' would have overcome its reactive mind and be cleared of all aberrations.

37, An OT is said to have complete control over life, thought, matter, energy, space, and time.

38-39, L. Ron Hubbard, THE ANTISOCIAL PERSONALITY THE ANTI-SCIENTOLOGIST, HCO POLICY LETTER OF 27 SEPTEMBER 1966

40, HCOB 23 Aug 1971 AUDITOR'S RIGHTS - AUDITORS DON'T HAVE CASES

41, Offensive term used in Scientology to speak about non-Scientologists.

42 43-44-45, CreateSpace Independent Publishing, Gillham Grady, Janis. Commodore's Messenger: A Child Adrift in the Scientology Sea Organization, Outback Publishing on to light up. And book 2: Riding Out The Storms with L. Ron Hubbard.

46, Atack, Jon. Let's sell these people A Piece of Blue Sky. Richard Woods

47, L. Ron Hubbard, THE ANTISOCIAL PERSONALITY THE ANTI-SCIENTOLOGIST, HCO POLICY LETTER OF 27 SEPTEMBER 1966

48, At times, depending on group influence and its level of the use of coercive persuasion and undue influence techniques, a cult member may drift in and out of altered states of consciousness or what has been called floating. See Ross, Rick. Cults Inside Out.

49, L. Ron Hubbard, Student Briefing, OT VIII Series I

50, Hyperalgesia is an abnormally increased sensitivity to pain.

51, www.ncbi.nlm.nih.gov/pmc/articles/PMC4186747/

52, www.tenspros.com/How-TENS-Units-Can-Help-Treat-Depression

53, https://neurolaunch.com/tens-for-anxiety/

54, The E-Meter Papers - How Does Scientology Auditing Work? (lermanet.org)

55, Scientists use high-tech brain stimulation to make people more hypnotizable | News Center | Stanford Medicine

56, Cults and the Mind-Body Connection, www.psychologytoday.com 215

57 58, https://croy.ulaval.ca/fiches/o/organisation-spirituelle-mondiale-brahma-kumaris

59, https://www.unadfi.org/groupes-et-mouvances/que-sait-on-de-brahma-kumaris/

60, https: //brahmakumaris.info/

Karen de la Carriere is one of the seven Level 12 case supervisors, the highest technician in Scientology.

www.ingramcontent.com/pod-product-compliance
Lightning Source LLC
Chambersburg PA
CBHW070545010526
44118CB00012B/1225